INTRODUCTION TO

BUSINESS LAW

JOHN LOK

Contents

Preface

Introduction

This book explains what are tort and criminal and contract law basic elements and indicates some case studies questions and suggests answers to let readers to know whether what are the tort and contract and competition law and criminal law contract law. It is suitable to any professionals to study , e.g. accountant, lawyer, doctor, architects , student. Readers can learn the basic law conept whether how any one citizen ought how to do to avoid any wrongdoing behavior in order to avoid to compensate any tort liability or criminal behavior. Also, any law students and professionals read this book can provide any basic tort and criminal and contract elements knowledge to let them to know.

Prologue

Table of content

Chapter five Law case research
(1) Sale of property case (contract law) p.51-65
(2) Breach of contract artist case
(3) Breach of contract artist case
(4) A share in the estate of the plaintiff's deceased father case (family law)
(5) Family law concerns shares owning authority in the name of plaintiff's deceased sister case
(6) Employment law, employee claims compensation for illness case.
(7) Family law, sex discrimination equal treatment case.
(8) Family law, who is divorce proceedings advisor case.
(9) Business law, suing bank compensation case.
(10) Breach sale of property contract claim to the firm of solicitors case.
(11) Employment contract and tort concerns worker's injury claim case.
(12) Applying the test, summary judgement application whether is dishonoured cheque claim case.

(13)Propery contract for occupy to earn profit unreal case

(14)The defendant (landload) lets premises to the plaintiff (rentee) case.

(15)Security for lawyer winner's cost case

(16)Employment contract, medical negligence claim case

(17)Wrongful dermination of an employment contract case.

(18) Cost orders of discovery of documents to whom lawyer's fee case

(19) Sale of cigarettes contract discovery of documents requested case.

(20) Discovery of document is not necessary case to flight case

(21) Discovery of cocuments, accident report at work case.

(22) Civil law process case

(23) Cost of litigation case

(24) Negligent claim case

(25) Breach of damage contract case

(26) Copyright infringerent claim civil case, product case

(27) Copyright infringerent claim drug civil compensation case

(28) Permanent injunction to the principles for a petrol filling station licence claim case

(29) Adequacy of damages to the plaintiff position case.

(30) Interrogatories witness evidence claim case

(31) Written evidence for sale a flat contract claim case

(32) Appeal process in written evidence injured compensation case.

(33) Weight of the evidence for employee's blood clot disease in an accident at working environment compensation case

(34) Seeking new evidence for dishonoured cheque defence case

(35) Extending the time limits relevant to

appeals the court of appeal for expert evidence case.

(36) Breach of copyright written evidence claim case.

(37) Defendant's video recorded for his interview with plaintiff unnecessary evidence claim case

CHAPTER I

Tort law basic elements questions

(1) Tortious acts many be classified in what ways?
Tort law refers to the set of laws that provides remedies to individuals who have suffered harm by the unreasonable acts of another. The law of tort is based on the idea that people are liable for the consequences of their actions, whether intentional or accidental,
if they cause harm to another person or entity. Torts are the civil wrongs that form the basis of civil lawsuits.
An area of law that deals with the wrongful actions of an individual or entity, which cause injury to another individual's or entity's person,
property, or reputation, and which entitle the injured party to compensation. They may include intentional tort refers , when a person intended the results or consequences of the act, e.g. assault, battery or false imprisonment; strict liability refers , when a person's conduct was neither intentional nor negligent, but is held liable wothout the plaintiff needs to prove fault; negligence refers when a person is careless, e.g. if a defendant decides to throws a stone at the plaintiff, the defendant has committed an intentional tort. But if the defendant intentionally throws a stone at a tree, buy misses and hits the plaintiff, the defendant may be negligent. Other torts included frequently enountered by the general public and include such acts as nuisance, occupier's liability, trespass and defamation.
Tort is conduct that harms other people or their property.

It is a private wrong against a person for which the injured person may recover damages, i.e. monetary compensation. The injured party may sue the wrongdoer (tortfeasor) to recover damages to compensate for the harm or loss incurred.

The conduct that is a tort may also be a crime. Some torts require intent before there will be liability and some torts require no intent. In other words, in some cases, there is liability for a tort even though the person committing the tort did not have any intent to do wrong.

● Types of Torts

There are basically three types of torts: intentional torts,torts based on negligence and strict liability torts. An intentional tort is a civil wrong that occurs when the wrongdoer engages in intentional conduct that results in damage to another. Striking another person in a fight is an intentional act that would be the tort of battery. Striking a person accidentally would not be an intentional tort since there was not intent to strike the person. This may, however, be a negligent act.

Careless conduct that results in damage to another is negligence. The intent element of these torts is satisfied when the tortfeasor acts with the desire to bring about harmful consequences and is substantially certain that such consequences will follow. Mere reckless behavior, sometimes called willful and wanton behavior, does not give rise to the level of an intentional tort.

If a person commits an intentional tort, this means that he intentionally violated a legal duty he owed to the victim. This is different from a negligent tort, in which the tortfeasor violated the duty that every member of society has to exercise reasonable care in their actions with others.

The distinction between an intentional tort and a negligent tort is important for several reasons.

First, if an individual wants to sue for an intentional tort, he must prove that the tortfeasor acted with "intent." This is a separate legal requirement that the plaintiff must fulfil, in addition to proving all the other facts of the case and proving actual damage. Strict liability, sometimes called absolute liability, is the legal responsibility for damage, or injury,

even if the person found strictly liable was not at fault or negligent – the injured party is not required to prove fault – liability is strict. An example of strict liability is injury caused by wild animals in the care of the tortfeasor; because the tortfeasor owns tigers, the tortfeasor is responsible for any injury, without the need for the injured party to prove negligence.

(2) What does tort of negligence mean?

The tort of negligence is the right to protect one's self and one's property from harm caused by the unreasonable behavior of another. Negligence is defined as careless or lack of proper care and attention in performing some act. A person is negligent as a tortfeasor, even if that person did not intend the consequences of the act (injury to another person or damage to another's property). It means that the tortfeasor was unaware of negligence of his action.

Negligence is as a tort m it is a breach of a legal duty to take care which results in damage to the claimant. It has four elements of negligence on a claim against a tortfeasor as below:

The defendant owes a duty of care to be injured party, i.e. a legal duty rather than a moral duty, the defendant must have breached the duty of care owed to the injured victim, who is bringing the claim to court, the victim's injury or damage must be caused by the defendant's breach of the duty of care, i.e. causation and the victim must suffer injury or damage.

(3) What does breath of duty of care mean?

It means that the conduct that falls below the standard regarded as normal as desirable. The special relationships may include: common carrier to passenger, innkeeper (hotel, motels) to guest, employer to employee, landowner or possessor to invitee, teacher to student, parent to child, hospital to patient, a professional person, such as a solicitor to client and lifeguard to swimmer. They have special duty of care roles to their clients.

The evaluate whether the defendent has breach of the suty of care. It depends on determining foreseeability factors as below:

Area in the location of the event and its physical nature, activity means the types of activities, which were present leading up to the event, people means the type of individuals involved in those activities, which lead up the event, human nature assumption means that the type of behavior which may be expected from those participating in the activities , participation means the anticipatory actions which were taken prior to the activities, historical data means where there was any prior knowledge of similar to identified occurrence and common sense factors.

● Duty of care

The defendant in a negligence action must have owed a legal duty of care to the claimant. There is a three-stage test to establish whether there was a duty of care:

· Is there a relationship of proximity between the parties?

· Was the injury to the claimant foreseeable?

· Is it fair, just and reasonable to impose a duty?

● Breach of duty

For the tort of negligence to have occurred, the defendant must have breached the duty of care legally imposed on them.The 'reasonable man' test is usually applied to ascertain whether the duty of care has been breached. This is a objective test, and considered whether the behaviour of the defendant fell below the threshold of a "reasonable man".

This will vary depending on the nature of the defendant. For instance, in a medical negligence case following a surgical procedure, the 'behaviour' – ie. the skills – of a specialist surgeon will be expected to be of a much higher standard than the skills of a junior doctor assisting. However, inexperience of itself will not be a valid defence: the defendant is expected to discharge his or her legal duty as a reasonably skilled and competent person.

● Causation

Once a breach of the legal duty of care has been established, it must be shown that the loss, damage or personal injury was caused
as a result, whether directly or indirectly. The question is: but for the actions or omission of the defendant, would the loss or harm have resulted?

● Harm or injury

There must be some form of loss, damage or injury. This includes physical or mental personal injuries; financial loss; or damage to
property. It can also extend to emotional distress or embarrassment.

(4) What does damage mean in tort of negligence?
Damage is the actual harm or loss suffered. Damages are the compensation which the injured party seeks from the tortfeasor. Damages frequently involve the issue of the actual amount of an injured party's financial loss. Generally, tort law is intended to make the injured party " whole" again, e.g. an award of damages is to serve as compensation for the losses.
What do damages mean in tort law ?
There are two types of damages recoverable, general and special damages both types. General damage is damage said to be the result of the tortious act complained of and need not be specified pleaded. Special damage means the particular damges, beyond the general damage, which results from the particular circumstances of the case.
Tort law is the body of laws that enables people to seek compensation for wrongs committed against them. When someone's actions cause some type
of harm to another, whether it be physical harm to another person, or harm to someone's property or reputation, the harmed or injured person or
entity may seek damages through the court.

Damages are a monetary award ordered by the court to be paid to an injured party, by the party at fault. Damages may be awarded in compensation for loss of, or damage to, personal or real property, for an injury, or for a financial loss. The types of damages that may be awarded by the court for civil wrongs, called "tortious conduct," of an individual or entity include: Reimbursement for property loss or property damage, medical expenses, pain and suffering, loss of earning capacity and punitive damages.

(5) How to denfence to the tort of negligence?
The tort law may involve both a civil case and a criminal

case resulting from the same act. IN a civil case, the burden of proving liability is lower than in a criminal case usually. The injured part in a civil case must prove all the element of the tort of negligence on the balance of probabilities standard. Otherwise, if the injured victim has failed to prove its case and the defendant is free of liability .

A tortfeasor may raise a defence which would relieve the tortfeasor from full or partial liability for the injury caused to the victim. Defences available to a tortfeasor against a claim of negligence are mainly contributory negligence and assumption of risk.

At common law, the defence os contributory negligence could completely prevent an injured victim's court action, provided that the victim was unreasonable in avoiding risks, and if this unreasonableness was a substantial factor in producing the injury. This would be the result, even if the defendant was also negligent.

On other words, if some contributory negligence could be shown on the injured victim's part, the victim would not be able to claim any damages in a negligence action. Assumption of risk means no injury is done to a person who consents to the risk of injury. It is a complete defence to an injured party's lawsuit. If a victim knowingly and voluntarily accepts the risks of injury by the defendant's negligence, the injured party can't recover for any loss, damage or injury . Courts generally interpret this denfence as courts are on policy to deny a victim of any compensation.

In addition, the concept of negligence has undergone significant reinterpretation over time, according to legal scholars. The law now takes into account the fact that manufacturers often have more ability than consumers to avoid accidents; thus, it is more likely to view failure to take

inexpensive action as negligence or
to attach liability to indirect or partial contribution to an injury.

(6) What may be included to tortious liabilities?

The legal term tort refers to an action in which one person or entity causes injury, harm, or damage to another person or entity. A tort liability may occur as a result of intentional acts, a negligent act, a failure to act when the individual had a duty to act, or a violation of statutes or laws. The individual who commits the tortious act (the act leading to the tort liability claim) is called the "tortfeasor," and is the defendant in this type of civil lawsuit. Such a defendant is generally held liable for damages or harm suffered by the plaintiff, as a result of the defendant's acts.

In many tort cases, the damages or injury suffered by the plaintiff do not have to be physical injury. A defendant in a tort liability case,
who is found to be liable for his or her tortious acts, may be ordered to pay damages for harm, such as violation of personal rights, pain and suffering, and emotional distress.

Tortious liabilities may include employer's liability, breach of statutory duty, employer's liability to workers, occupier's liability, nurisance, trespass, defamation.
Vicarious liability is legal responsibility imposed on a person for the torts of others, regardless of any fault on the part of the non-tortfeasor. Vicarious liability generally arises from an employer and employee relationship and is conceptually similar to strict liability in tort.
Under vicarious liability , an employer's liability does not depend upon the employer's person fault. Rather, an employer is strictly liable for an employee's negligent acts performed of employment . The requirements for vicarious liability are the tortfeasor is hired by the employer as an

employee , the employee committed the tortious act, the employee's tortious act was in connection with, or employment, e.g. employer's liability for independent contractors. IN general , employers are not liable for torts committed by their independent contractors. The most basic principle is that an employer is not liable for an independent contractor's negligence, provided always the contractor employed is one reasonably supposed by the employer to be competent.

Trespass is unlike negligence, involves an intentional act. Trespassory tort, such as trespass to the person or trespass to land, are less frequently than the negligence-based torts. Then committed this type of tort often is also a crime for which the wrongdoes is imprisoned. Acts such as murder and rape are examples of trepass to the person, but are usually only dealt with as criminal acts by courts. Therefore, an injured party would not bother with the inconvenience of a civil action, although the right to sue exists, e.g. hospital negligent medical treatment to patients case.

Defamation is a tort action for the protection of one's reputation to establish defamation, a plaintiff has to prove that the defendant has published (or is reponsible for the publication of) defamatory material that is reasonably understood to refer to plaintiff. Tort law protects a person's reputation from damage or injury by defamatory statements, of and concerning the plaintiff and published to a third-party or parties.

Tort liability can be imposed in many instances that include negligent behaviour towards a person or land, negatively affecting a person's reputation

or limiting freedom of movement. This module will aim to explain and take you through how and why liability can be imposed on a defendant, giving you and in-depth understanding of the nature of tortious liability.

There are many torts that will be discussed in this module. They include, for example, libel, slander, nuisance, negligence, trespass, assault and battery. Thus, it is not possible to provide one definition that encompasses all torts, considering how each tort has its own specific characteristics.

It is, therefore, best to think of the law of tort as the law of behaviour that is legally 'wrong' or 'tortious', giving rise to an entitlement to a remedy for the claimant.

Whilst it may not be possible to precisely define what tort is, various principles can be identified that help establish when a tortious liability arises. It has to be noted, however, that there is no predominance of any one principle. The principles that can be turned to are:

- Compensation
- Fault
- Retributive justice (punishment)
- Deterrence
- Economic efficiency
- Loss distribution

Tort law also aims to protect individual interests from a harm that is actual or threatened. However, not all interests are protected and some benefit from better protection than others. This is as a result of the importance of an interest reflected by society through the years. The interests protected include: Personal harm , harm to property ,harm to reputation ,harm to financial interests and harm to the due process of law.

(7) What are types of tort liabilities ?

There are a number of specific types of tort liabilities that form the basis of the majority of civil lawsuits in the United States. These include, among others: Negligence, intentional Infliction of emotional distress, assault, battery,trespass, products liability.

Tort law divides most specific torts into three general categories:

1.Intentional Torts – the causing of harm by an intentional act, such as intentionally conning someone out of his money.

2.Negligent Torts – the causing of harm through some negligent act, such as causing a car accident by running a red light.

3.Strict Liability Torts – the result of harm incurred due to the actions of another, with no finding of fault by the defendant.

The additional and separate specific torts include:
Defamation Torts, Nuisance Torts, Privacy Torts
and Economic Torts

(1) Intentional torts are acts committed with the intent to harm another, or to deliberately interfere with an individual's rights to bodily safety,
emotional tranquility, privacy, control over property, freedom from deception, and freedom from confinement. Intentional torts commonly include such issues as assault and/or battery, false imprisonment, invasion of privacy, theft, property damage, fraud or other deception, and trespassing.

Intent is a key issue in proving an intentional tort, as the injured party, called the Plaintiff, must prove to the court that the other party,
called the Respondent or Defendant, acted intentionally, and knew that his actions could cause harm. In some cases,

the Plaintiff need only prove that the Defendant should have known that his actions could cause harm. Many intentional torts may also be charged as criminal offenses.

Intentional tort case examples:

Johnny stops by the local bar for a few drinks before he heads home after work. After drinking four cocktails, Raymond gets into his car, and runs
a stop sign, crashing into another car, seriously injuring its occupants. Although Johnny might argue that he didn't know he would hurt someone,
it is expected that Johnny should have known that driving under the influence is likely to cause harm, or to kill another person.Because Johnny intentionally drank alcohol, knowing he planned on driving home, and any reasonable person should know that drinking and driving could result in harm, he has committed an intentional tort. In addition, Johnny may be criminally charged with .

(2) Negligent Torts

The acts leading to claims of harm or injury in negligent torts are not intentional. There are three specific elements that must be satisfied in a claim of negligence:

1.The defendant must have a duty or owe a service to the plaintiff or victim

2.The defendant must have failed that duty, or violated a promise or obligation to the plaintiff

3.The plaintiff must have suffered an actual loss, injury, or damages that were directly caused by the plaintiff's actions, or failure to act

(3) Strict Liability Torts

Strict liability refers to the concept of imposing liability on a defendant, usually a manufacturer, without proving negligent fault, or intent to cause harm. The purpose of strict liability torts is to regulate activities that are acknowledged as being necessary and useful to society, but which pose an abnormally high risk of danger to the public.

Such activities may include transportation and storage of hazardous substances, blasting, and keeping certain wild animals in captivity.

The possibility of civil lawsuits under strict liability torts keeps individuals or corporations undertaking such dangerous acts diligent in

taking every possible precaution to keep the public safe.

(4) Suing Under Strict Liability Tort

In a strict liability lawsuit, the law assumes that the supplier or manufacturer of the product was aware the defect existed before the product

reached the consumer. Because of this, the plaintiff need only prove that harm or damages occurred, and that the defendant is responsible.

To successfully bring a civil lawsuit under a strict liability tort, the following elements must be proven:

1.The named defendant is the manufacturer of the defective product.

2.The product was defective when the plaintiff purchased it.

3.The defect was present when the defendant sold the product.

4.The defect caused the plaintiff's injuries or damages.

5.The injuries or damages caused by the product's defect were reasonably foreseeable by the defendant.

A plaintiff in a strict liability lawsuit may be awarded additional damages if he can prove that the defendant knew about the defect when the product was sold to consumers.

Suing Under Strict Liability Tort case example:

Peter buys a new car from local Auto dealership. Only three months later, The car dealership noticed Peter brakes felt soft, so the car dealership took peter car to dealer's repair shop. They told peter just needed new brake pads, replaced them, and sent the auto car dealership on her way. A month later, while Peter was driving on a busy freeway, Peter brakes failed, and Peter crashed into another car. Peter's car was very badly damaged, and Peter suffered a broken arm and a concussion.

Peter discovers, while researching the brake problem Peter had been having with his car, that this particular model has had brake problems
since it was first released for sale to the public. In digging deeper, The car dealer discovers that Zoom Auto knew the car's brake system was
defective before they sold the cars, but determined it would be too expensive to bring them all back into the factory to change out the brake systems.

In suing Zoom Auto, The car dealer must use this information to prove:

1.Zoom Auto manufactured the defective vehicle.

2.The car's brake system was defective when she bought the car.

3.The car's brake system was defective when Zoom Auto sold the car to Peter.

4.The brake defect caused Peter's injuries, as well as the severe damage to her car.

5.It was reasonably foreseeable that selling a car with a defective brake system would cause injury to consumers.

6.Zoom Auto knew about the defective brake system in this particular model car before they sold the vehicles, yet chose to sell them anyway,
in blatant disregard of the safety of consumers.

Under the Federal Tort Claims Act ("FTCA"), the U.S.

government is liable for the tortious acts of individuals acting on the government's behalf,
in the same way a private party would be liable in similar circumstances. The amount of damages that may be awarded in such a lawsuit, however,
is limited, with no allowance for punitive damages, or interest accumulated prior to the date of judgment.

The FTCA specifies that anyone wishing to file a tort claim against the United States must do so, in writing to the appropriate federal agency,
within two years of the date the tort occurred. This means that the statute of limitations on filing an administrative claim under the FTCA is two years.

Any individual wishing to file an administrative claim for reimbursement for damages or injury must demonstrate that:

1.His property was damaged, or he was injured, by the actions of an employee of the federal government.

2.The federal employee was acting in his official capacity at the time the damage or injury occurred.

3.The federal employee acted wrongfully, or negligently.

4.The federal employee's wrongful or negligent act caused the plaintiff's damages or injury.

In most tort cases, an individual who desires to file a claim under the FTCA must first file an administrative claim with the federal agency
that employs the employee that caused the damages. This requires filling out the required forms, and providing documents or other evidence
supporting the claimant's position. Forms and additional information can be obtained from the Department of Justice website.

Once an administrative claim has been filed, the agency has six months to respond to the claimant. If the claimant is not happy with the agency's response or decision, he has six months from the date the response was mailed to him to file a civil lawsuit under the FTCA. In the event the federal agency does not respond to the claimant within the six month time frame, the claimant may go ahead and file a civil lawsuit, but his six-month statute of limitations does not begin to run until the agency actually provides a response or decision. When filing a claim under the FTCA, the lawsuit must be filed in the U.S. District Court, which is the official name of the federal court, in the district where the tortious act occurred, or where the plaintiff lives.

(5) trespass and false imprisonment

Trespass

A trespass is an unauthorized action with respect to a person or property. A trespass to the person consists of any contact with someone's person for which consent was not given. This is technically described as a battery. An assault would be a situation where a plaintiff reasonably believed a battery upon his person was about to be committed. An example of an assault would be where one person swings his fist at another person. If the person made contact, this would be an assault and battery. A defense to assault and battery would be in cases of self-defense.

A trespass to land involves going on or above the property of another without permission. A trespass can also involve the unpermitted use of the airspace of another's property as well as actually going on the actual property. However, this rule has been modified to allow the flight of aircraft above the land as long as it does not interfere with the proper use of the land.

A trespass to personal property is the use of someone's property without the person's permission.

A conversion occurs when personal property is taken by a defendant and kept from its true owner

without permission of the owner. Conversion is the civil side of the crime of theft. The concept is based on the tortfeasor converting something to their own use. It also requires an intention to deprive the true owner of their ownership – so if you put a mobile in your pocket thinking it was

yours it would not be conversion.

False Imprisonment

False imprisonment involves detaining a person without that person's consent. It can take the extreme form of kidnapping or the less extreme form of detaining a shopper for suspected shoplifting without reasonable grounds.

A defense to false imprisonment would be consent of the detainee, or if a store owner had reasonable grounds to believe that the detainee was guilty of shoplifting (shopkeeper's privilege). This privilege allows a store owner (or his employee) to detain a suspected shoplifter based on reasonable suspicion for a reasonable time.

A customer was shopping at the handbag counter of the defendant's store. She did not make any purchase and left the store. When she was a few feet outside the store, an employee of the store tapped her lightly on the shoulder to attract her attention and asked her if she had made any

purchase. When she inquired why, the employee asked, "What about that bag in your hand?" The

customer said that it belonged to her and she opened it to show by its contents that it was not a new bag. The employee gave the customer a "real dirty look" and went back into the store without saying a word. The customer then sued the store for false imprisonment. Was the store liable? No.

Judgment would be for the store. There was no false imprisonment because there was no actual detaining of the customer. The circumstances did not show the use of force or threat of force that stopped the customer from proceeding on her way. Her action of stopping and showing the contents of her handbag was voluntary.

(6) negligence and malpractice

Negligence is a failure to follow the degree of care that would be followed by a reasonably prudent person in order to avoid foreseeable harm. A person can be negligent if he or she acts with less care than a reasonable person would use under similar circumstances.

Bob drove a car on a country road at 35 miles an hour. The maximum speed limit was 45 miles an hour. He struck and killed a cow that was crossing the road. The owner of the cow sued Bill for the value of the cow. Bill said that since he was not driving above the speed limit, there could be no liability for negligence. Was this defense valid? No. A person must at all times act in the manner in which a reasonable person would act under the circumstances. The fact that Bill was driving within the speed limit was only one of the circumstances to consider. The weather or the condition of the road may have made it unreasonable to drive at 35 miles an hour. Driving slower than the speed limit does not in and of itself prove that the driver was acting reasonably.

The reasonable person standard varies in accordance with the situation. The degree of care required of a person is that which an ordinarily prudent person would exercise under similar circumstances. This does not necessarily mean a degree of care that would have prevented the harm from occurring.

The elements required to establish negligence are: the presence of duty; a voluntary act or failure to act (an omission) that breaches the duty; proximate causation of harm; and damage (i.e., the breach of duty causes harm to the plaintiff).

Torts involve duties created by law. Just because someone is hurt does not mean that someone else must pay for the harm. There must have been a duty which has been breached. A plaintiff will not be allowed to recover from a defendant if the defendant did not breach a duty that was owed to the plaintiff. For example, if a burglar breaks into my house and trips over an item of furniture, I am not liable to the burglar because I had no duty to him. However, if a guest in my house trips over a piece of furniture, I may have a duty to that guest. The breach of duty must result from a voluntary act or failure to act.

In order for someone to be legally responsible for damage, it is necessary to show that the wrongful act was the proximate cause of the harm. The injury must be shown to be the natural and probable result or consequence of the alleged act of negligence. The plaintiff must prove that the defendant's negligence proximately caused the Plaintiff's injury. There may be more than one proximate cause of an accident.

The final element of negligence is damages. A plaintiff may recover monetary damages to compensate the plaintiff for economic losses such as lost wages and medical expenses. A plaintiff may also recover non-economic losses such as for pain and suffering. The former are claimed on a normal accounting basis, and the latter are at the discretion of the judge.

(7) Malpractice

Malpractice is a failure by a physician or other professional to use the skill and care that other members of their profession would use under similar circumstances. When an accountant, doctor, attorney, or some other professional contracts to perform services, there is a duty to exercise skill and care as is common within the community for persons performing similar services. Failure to fulfil that duty is malpractice.

(8) Nuisance

Nuisance is a civil wrong, consisting of anything wrongfully done or permitted that interferes with or annoys others in the enjoyment of their legal rights. It is anything that annoys or disturbs the free use of one's property or that renders its ordinary use or physical occupation uncomfortable.

A nuisance is anything that interferes with the rights of citizens, the enjoyment of their property, or their comfort. It is to be noted that an unreasonable interference with another person's use and enjoyment of his/her property is determined by the injury caused by the condition and is not determined by the conduct of the party creating the condition.

A nuisance is differentiated from a trespass to land. A trespass is an invasion of a person's interest in the exclusive possession of their land, whereas a nuisance is an interference with the use and enjoyment of the land and does not require interference with the possession. A person injured by a nuisance can recover damages in an action at law for tort. Similarly, damages can also be recovered for injury resulting from the legal use of a property, if such use substantially damages the property of another.

Nuisances are divided into different subheads such as nuisances per se, public or common nuisances, private nuisances, etc. A public nuisance exists when an act or condition is subversive of public order or constitutes an obstruction of public rights. In other words, a public nuisance involves an unreasonable interference with a right common to the general public. In order to constitute a public nuisance, it is not necessary that it affects the whole community. It is a public nuisance if the injury or annoyance affects the people of a local neighborhood. Public nuisances always arise out of unlawful acts.

Therefore, acts that are lawful or authorized by a valid statute, or which the public convenience demands, cannot be a public nuisance. A public nuisance can constitute either a crime or may be the subject of a civil action by public officials or private individuals. At common law, the term "public nuisance" covers a variety of minor criminal offenses that interfer, for example, with the public health, safety, morals, peace, or convenience. Public nuisances include for example, a manufacturer who has polluted a stream and might be fined and be ordered to pay the cost of cleanup. Public safety nuisances include shooting fireworks in the streets or storing explosives.

A private nuisance is a civil wrong that affects a single individual or a definite number of persons in the enjoyment of some private right which is not common to the public. In other words, a private nuisance is a substantial and unreasonable interference with the private use and enjoyment of one's land. Examples include interference with the physical condition of the land, disturbing the comfort of its occupants, or threatening injury or disturbance in the future.

Nuisances that interfere with the physical condition of the land include vibration or blasting that damages a house; destruction of crops; raising of a water table; or the pollution of soil, a stream, or an underground water supply. Examples of nuisances interfering with the comfort, convenience, or health of an occupant are foul odors, noxious gases, smoke, dust, loud noises, excessive light, or high temperatures, e.g. a landowner burning plastic and old tyres so that the smell and smoke affect his neighbours.

(9) Defamation

Defamation is the communication of a false statement that harms the reputation of an individual. The law of defamation protects a person's reputation and good name against communications that are false and derogatory. Defamation consists of two torts: libel and slander. Libel consists of any defamation that can be seen, most typically in writing. Slander is a form of defamation that consists of making false oral statements about a person which would damage that person's reputation. If I spread a rumor that my neighbor has been in jail and this is not true, I could be held liable for slander.

A person is liable for the defamation of another. In order to prove defamation, the plaintiff must prove:

- that a statement was made about the plaintiff's reputation, honesty or integrity that is not true;
- there was publication to a third party (i.e., another person hears or reads the statement); and
- the plaintiff suffers damage as a result of the statement.

Public figures have a more difficult time proving defamation. Politicians or celebrities are understood to take some risk in being in the public eye and many of them profit by their public persona. A celebrity must prove that the party defaming them knew the statements were false, made them with actual malice (intent to harm), or was negligent in saying or writing them. Proving these elements can be an uphill battle. However, an outrageously inaccurate statement that's harmful to one's career can be grounds for a successful defamation suit, even if the subject is famous. For example, some celebrities have won suits against tabloids for false statements regarding their ability to work, such as an inaccurate statement that the star had a drinking problem.

Another important aspect of defamation is the difference between fact and opinion. Statements made as "facts" are frequently actionable defamation. Statements of opinion or pure opinion are not actionable. Some jurisdictions decline to recognize any legal distinction between fact and opinion. To win damages in a libel case, the plaintiff must first show that the statements were "statements of fact or mixed statements of opinion and fact" and second that these statements were false.

Conversely, a typical defense to defamation is that the statements are opinion. One of the major tests to distinguish whether a statement is fact or opinion is

whether the statement can be proved
true or false in a court of law. If the statement can be proved true or false, then, on that basis, the
case will be heard by a jury to determine whether it is true or false. For example, your statement of
opinion is just an opinion, and does not contain specific facts that can be proved untrue. "The waiters and waitresses at the Tivoli Restaurant are too slow and the food is too spicy." This is a statement of opinion. "I got food poisoning at the Tivoli Restaurant" is potentially a defamatory statement if, in fact, the restaurant can prove that you never contracted food poison."

Some statements, while libelous or slanderous, are absolutely privileged in the sense that the statements can be made without fear of a lawsuit for slander. The best example is a statement made in a court of law. An untrue statement made by a witness about a person in court which damages that person's reputation will generally not be held to be liability to the witness as far as slander is concerned.

(10) Strict liability torts and Vicarious liability

Strict Liability

Strict or absolute liability is the legal responsibility for damage or injury, even if the person found strictly liable was not at fault. In order to prove strict liability in tort, plaintiff needs to prove only that the tort happened and that the defendant was responsible for the act or omission.

In the case of strict liability in the USA, neither good faith nor the fact that the defendant took all possible precautions is a valid defense. A common example of strict liability is imposing product liability in the case of defectively manufactured products.

Strict liability applies especially in cases involving hazardous or dangerous activities.

Generally, liability based on a tort only arises where the defendant either intended to cause harm to the plaintiff or in situations where the defendant is negligent. However, in some areas, liability can arise even when there is no intention to cause harm or negligence. For example, when a contractor uses dynamite which causes debris to be thrown onto the land of another and damages a landowner's house, the landowner may recover damages from the contractor even if the contractor was not negligent and did not intend to cause any harm. Basically, society is saying that the activity is so dangerous to the public that there must be liability. However, society is not going so far as to outlaw the activity.

Example: Acme Construction Company was constructing a highway. It was necessary to blast rock with dynamite. The corporation's employees did this with the greatest of care. In spite of their precautions, some flying fragments of rock damaged a neighboring house. The owner of the house sued the corporation for damages. The corporation raised the defense that the owner was suing for tort damages and that such damages could not be imposed because the corporation had been free from fault. Was this defense valid? No. While ordinarily fault is the basis of tort liability, there are cases in which absolute liability is imposed on the actor. This means that when harm is caused, it is no defense that none was intended or that due care had been exercised to prevent the harm.

Other examples of absolute liability situations would be harm caused by storage of flammable gas and explosives, factories which produce dangerous fumes or smoke in populated areas, and the production of nuclear material.

Vicarious liability is the responsibility of the superior for the acts of their subordinate. It is the responsibility of a third party who has the right, ability or duty to control the activities of a violator.

Typically liability flows from the relationship of master and servant. The relationship includes the
power to direct the servant in the execution of the duties of his/her employment, and to control the
acts that no injury is done to third persons.
An employer can be held vicariously liable for an employee's tortious act against the person or property of a third party in a transaction of the employer's business. If a negligent act is committed by an employee acting within the general scope of her or his employment, the employer will be held liable for damages. For example, if the driver of a gasoline delivery truck runs a red light on the way to a gas station and strikes another car, causing injury, the gasoline delivery company will be responsible for the damage if the driver is found to be negligent.

(9) Why do some countries feel need to reform
tort law?
For US government tort law system example, Some American citizen feels needs to reform tort law in US. I shall indicate reasons as below:

In US tort law system, the term tort reform has been bandied about as a hot-button issue since the congressional elections in 2010. The average American citizen does not understand what tort reform actually means, and has no idea that it has no bearing on any laws, but is a general acknowledgement that the amount of damages awarded to victorious plaintiffs in tort lawsuits has grown too large.

In past decades, juries have sought to sufficiently reimburse plaintiffs for tortious wrongs committed against

them, as well as to punish
many defendants for actions the jury considers. Many proposed tort reform acts have proven to be ill considered, however, as they seek to make it more difficult for people to file civil lawsuits, to make it more difficult for plaintiffs to obtain a jury trial on a civil matter, and to cap the amount of money plaintiffs can be awarded in various types of civil lawsuits.

While some people consider awards made to certain victorious plaintiffs, the truth is, some of these plaintiffs experience seriously increased costs of living, medical expenses, loss of income, and loss of quality of life, due to the tortious behaviors of others. An award of damages in the millions of dollars range may sound like a large award, but when considering it spread over the plaintiff's lifetime, it is often merely enough to get by.

● Mc Donald's tort negligent wrongdoing behavior to compensate big compensation sue amount case:

Tort reform has come under public awareness, as many people find publicized awards in civil lawsuits to be shockingly large. One of the most
famous tort lawsuits in recent history in the case of a 79-year old woman who sued McDonald's restaurants when she spilled her coffee, and was burned.

Liebeck v. McDonald's Restaurants sue compensation case:

In 1992, 79-year old Stella Liebeck spilled a cup of McDonald's coffee in her lap, sustaining third degree burns to both legs. The severity of
the full-thickness burns required skin grafts. This involved stripping skin from other areas of Liebeck's body to graft onto the burned areas
which were no longer able to grow skin on their own,

leaving her with even more wounds to heal.

When McDonald's denied Liebeck's request to pay her medical bills, she filed a civil lawsuit.

During the course of the case, it was discovered McDonald's had received hundreds of other complaints from customers complaining that their

coffee had caused severe burns, and that the corporation's operations manual specified the coffee was to be kept at 180-190 degrees Fahrenheit. It is known and accepted, by the scientific and medical communities, that liquid at that temperature, if spilled onto a person, causes third degree burns in three to seven seconds.

A jury awarded Liebeck $200,000 in compensatory damages to pay for medical bills and other related expenses. Because it was clear the company knew its coffee was kept at a dangerously high temperature, and was therefore likely cause serious injury, the jury also awarded Liebeck $2.7 million in punitive damages, which amounted to the company's sales revenue from just two days of coffee sales.

While many proponents of tort reform view this case as a supreme example of a frivolous lawsuit with a shockingly high award, the truth is, McDonald's knew its coffee could cause third degree burns, yet continued to specifically instruct its restaurant employees to keep and serve

it at that temperature. Ms. Liebeck's injuries were severe, her painful third degree burns requiring skin grafts. McDonald's was given an opportunity to settle the matter out of court, but they refused to do so.

To judge this case relates whether McDonald ought need to compensate to the old woman or not? It depends on these related Legal Terms and Issues as these factors below:

Civil Lawsuit – A lawsuit brought about in court when one person claims to have suffered a loss due to the actions of another person.

Criminal Offense – An act committed by an individual that is in violation of the law, or that poses a threat to the public.

Damages – A monetary award in compensation for a financial loss, loss of or damage to personal or real property, or an injury.

Defendant – A party against whom a lawsuit has been filed in civil court, or who has been accused of, or charged with, a crime or offense.

Entity – An individual, company, association, trust, or other organization that is legally recognized in the eyes of the law. A legal entity
is able to enter into contracts, take on obligations, pay debts, be sued, and be held responsible for its actions.

Personal Property – Any item that is moveable and not fixed to real property.

Plaintiff – A person who brings a legal action against another person or entity, such as in a civil lawsuit, or criminal proceedings.

Punitive Damages – Money awarded to the injured party above and beyond their actual damages. Punitive damages, also referred to as "exemplary
damages," are ordered for the purpose of punishing the wrongdoer for outrageous misconduct in a civil matter.

Real Property – Land and property attached or fixed directly to the land, including buildings and structures.

Ultimately, the judge reduced the amount awarded by the jury to $640,000, and the case was appealed by McDonald's, which finally settled for an undisclosed amount before the appeal concluded. In this case, the current tort system worked property, as it prompted McDonald's to settle the case, quite possibly because of a concern that the award would be boosted back up to the original amount awarded by the jury. However, the final result. McDonald does not need to compensate to this old woman when she sues the accident compensation. The severity of the full-thickness burns required skin grafts. This involved stripping skin from other areas of Liebeck's body to graft onto the burned areas which were no longer able to grow skin on their own, leaving her with even more wounds to heal.

In conclusion, due to the compensation is too much, so it is unreasonable compensation amout to sue McDonald needs to pay to this old woman client's body hurt claim. However, US court still need McDonald to compensate part body hurt loss to this old woman client's accident claim for her stripping skin from other areas of Liebeck's body to graft onto the burned areas which were no longer able to grow skin on their own, leaving her with even more wounds to heal. So, it explains why US tort law needs to be reformed again, such as this compensation amout is too much and unfair and unreasonable to this McDonald's accident body hurt to this old woman client's case.

● Why is tort reform necessary in the United States?

Tort reform is necessary in the US because insurance companies, big business, big pharma
and big medical interests, and unscrupulous irresponsible entities and persons need the protection of the courts and laws so they can make more obscene profits and face little or no risk when they cause harm to people through their negligence and intentional acts that a jury determines are reasonably forseeable to cause harm. And do not believe a

jury acts without restraint. The trial judge can dismiss cases before they get to the jury or set aside unsupportable jury verdicts. Appeals courts can also reverse trial results that are
unreasonable. Hence, big business is now spending many millions of dollars getting judges they support elected to the highest courts in the various states, where their pro-big business interests can be furthered. Years ago, these
state judge races were not fueled by such enormous funding.

Many tort reform promoters want our laws to abandon its position in protecting the people from harm intentionally or negligently caused by others. Lets limit the damages these wrongdoers can be accessed. Lets limit legal fees and damage
awards on medical malpractice and elder care neglect cases so lawyers will not be able to accept all but the most extreme cases of wrongdoing. Alot of people think they support tort reform until it is their parent or child or themselves who suffered injury due to someones wanton or reckless act. Some of these reform supporters bought into the idea of lower insurance insurance premiums or lower medical costs promised in return for tort reform laws passed. I suggest they were sold a lie.

Of course, tort reform is necessary in the US because the Constitutional right of people to seek redress of wrongs against them in the courts, including their constitutional rights to a jury, equal protection under the law, and so many protections you can find in our Constitution and Bill of Rights, hinder business profits and cost big pharma too much money to properly warn people of the dangerous side effects of their drugs, they knew about. Is not progress and profit more important than corporate accountability?

● The Absolute Need for Tort Reform

I'm planning on looking at various problems liberals whine and complain about needing more government and show how each and everyone one of those problems is caused in multiple ways by more government. And I already know that in in most of the cases it's going to come back to Tort Reform being needed, so I figured I should put together some evidence for it.

Tort Reform? Tort law is the law that governs civil lawsuits. Right now the Democratic Party (and quite a few RINOs) as a wholly owned subsidiary of the American Bar Association (read unethical scum and ambulance chasers) are against tort reform (probably because it would be good for the nation).

However reforms like limiting the amounts you can receive for pain and suffering, limiting lawsuits to negligence or the but-for test (where you can sue unless you can prove but for the plaintiff's actions the defendant would be fine),

creating a loser pays system (where the loser has to pay the winner's legal fees), penalties for ambulance chasers who bring in one frivolous lawsuit after another, and more power for judges to throw out frivolous cases. Simple things like that.

This may all sound silly, or even pointless. But take a look at the warning labels on items when you buy them. Almost all of these are because stupid people used these items in an inappropriate way...and then they sued. And when the

company they sued loses the costs hurt you either by raised prices or fewer employees being hired.

Even when the company doesn't win, they've still lost because of legal fees. And you still bear the burden of the cost. All because stupid people also happen to be litigious people (also because lawyers tend to be somewhere on the evolutionary chain below pond scum).

Every state that has engaged in tort reform has seen lower costs, more employment, fewer court costs and more efficient courts, a stimulated economy and more tax revenue. They've even seen fewer deaths because doctors aren't afraid anymore to actually practice medicine.

Tort reform is primarily a state by state issue, and you should see where your state is in terms of tort laws and if you have time try and get tort reform in your state. However there are also a few federal issues (as there are federal civil

cases) and thus we need some federal reform as well. But don't believe me. Here is a body of op-eds, reports, studies and opinions by people who have done far more research than I.

It all comes to the same conclusion, we need tort reform.

1. Most cases aren't civil lawsuits so this isn't a problem.

That's because most companies will settle because they know juries are unreliable and composed of 12 people too dumb to get out of jury duty.

Thus most things that come under the law governed by tort law are handled out of court.

2. Evil corporations want tort reform.

Any time the whole argument is against corporations, you know it's a BS argument. Corporations can be good or bad depending on their behavior. Corporations will actually behave better when only legitimate lawsuits are brought against them and we don't knee jerk dismiss every lawsuit as the work of an ambulance chaser.

3. Tort reform limits people from receiving their right to a jury trial. Juries are one of the most basic defenses of a democracy.

First we live in a republic, a system designed on the premise that people are fickle and can be stupid. And for anyone who wants to plead the intelligence of juries I have two letters for you: OJ. Juries are a last ditch effort that no one wants, it's why so many criminal cases are plead out, and so many civil suits dealt with out of court. Juries are at best unpredictable and at worst consistently illogical . They're trying to make a pointless emotional argument that has nothing to do with facts.

4. Tort reform will limit the amount that people have a right to when they are harmed by people and corporations.

The only thing I know we want to limit is "pain and suffering" costs. If you're a professional athlete and have your body injured by a corporation you could still sue them for loss of income for millions. But that doesn't often happen. It's pain and suffering judgments that create the most in awards and it's these that are often the most ridiculous.

5. Injured people will not be able to file suit if we have tort reform.

Actually since there will be fewer frivolous lawsuits from ambulance chasers throwing everything against a wall to see what sticks, people with real cases (but who don't have sleazy lawyers who know how to work the field) will have a better chance of getting their case heard.

(10) What is the tort law system difference between US and UK ?

In U.S. tort legal system, U.S. tort law is based primarily on common law—in which judicial rules are developed on a case-by-case basis by trial judges—rather than on legislation. Tort liability is assigned using two basic standards: strict liability and negligence. Under strict liability, injurers are held fully liable for their victims' losses without regard for whether they were actually negligent or intended to harm anyone.

Under a negligence standard, by contrast, injurers are held liable only if they failed to meet a certain standard of care. According to legal scholars, a number of important developments have increased the scope of liability for torts in the United States.

Otherwise, in UK legal system, early English tort law, the antecedent of U.S. tort law, was chiefly concerned with making injurers pay for the losses of their victims, with little emphasis on fault or negligence. That standard was used in the United States until the 19th century, when U.S. common law established negligence as the basis for tort liability. However, strict liability continued to apply in certain cases, such as injuries caused by wild animals kept as pets or damage to crops caused by trespass of domestic animals.3 Some scholars argue that the requirement for plaintiffs to show that defendants had been negligent effectively limited the scope of the U.S. tort system.

The 20th century saw public policy increasingly emphasize victim compensation and accident reduction. The enactment of workers' compensation laws— which established a public insurance system aimed at lowering employers' payments while making workers' recovery of damages automatic—played an important role in the evolution of tort law and policy. Before workers' compensation programs, the only remedy that injured workers had was to prove their employers negligent through the tort system. Workers favored legislation instead because they often had been unable to recover damages or had experienced delays or high costs when they had been successful. For their part, employers favored legislation because it limited their liability and made payments predictable.That shift away from tort law to a public compensation system led to more thought about how tort liability could be improved or better applied in other types of cases.

By the 1940s, legal scholars had begun to think about two ways in which the tort system could serve the wider goal of enhancing social welfare. First, they saw the economic concept of "cost internalization" as a tool for reducing accident rates: if potential injurers know they will be held liable for accidents, they will take appropriate action to avoid liability. In that view, by awarding damages to compensate victims, tort law would serve as a mechanism to ensure that potential injurers faced the appropriate future costs of their actions. Second, some scholars argued that the tort system could provide a kind of accident insurance for victims. They did not focus on the possibility that an expanded liability system could increase carelessness on the part of potential victims, nor did they adopt any of the methods that traditional insurance policies use to deal with that problem. Rather, they focused exclusively on the distributional goal of relieving victims of the burden of accident losses and spreading that burden across a broader population.

For UK legal system practice was product liability. Historically, product liability was dealt with either as a breach of warranty under contract law or as a tort subject to the negligence standard. Under contract law, recovery in such cases was limited to repair and replacement of the product; under tort law, recovery was limited by the difficulty of proving negligence. It is different to US product liability act.

In the 1960s, the courts moved rapidly toward a standard of strict liability for defective products; in 1964, that standard was accepted and recommended by the American Law Institute in its second Restatement of the Law volume
on torts. By the mid-1970s, most states had adopted provisions that were either identical or similar to those in the Restatement.

What is a tort to UK ?

The law of tort is wide-ranging body of rights, obligations and remedies applied by the courts in civil proceedings.
It provides remedies relief for those who have suffered loss or harm following the wrongful or negligent acts of others.

A tort is a civil wrong by the 'tortfeasor' that unfairly results in loss or harm to another. This makes the tortfeasor liable to the other. Tort is distinguishable from two other kinds of law – criminal law and contract law, and is dealt with by the civil courts.

Unlike tort, the criminal law are wrongs against society and is comprised in legislation and prosecuted by the authorities,
and dealt with in the criminal courts. In contract law, the rights and obligations between the contractual parties are governed by the contract itself and not by the law of tort.

However, sometimes the line is blurred between tort, crime and contract law. For instance, violent offences against the person
such as assault and battery can be prosecuted by the Crown;

and a damages claim can also be brought in the civil courts by the victim.

● Parties to an action in tort

Anyone can sue in tort if they suffered harm or loss as a result of someone else's civil wrong. There is the potential for children to sue,
including children who are born with disabilities due to harm inflicted prior to birth; and even a husband and wife can sue each other.

Claimants can sue a wide range of tortfeasor. The following are examples of different types of individuals and other parties who can
potentially face an action against them under the law of tort:

- Individuals
- The Crown
- Companies
- Employers
- Employees
- Independent contractors
- Occupiers of premises
- Individuals who have caused damage to another's reputation
- Dangerous drivers
- Individuals in the medical profession
- Occupiers of recreational premises

What are the elements of the Law of Tort?

Negligence

Whilst there are different types of tort, negligence is by far the most common tort for which claimants take legal action.
There are four elements to the tort of negligence. Each of

these must be present for a claim to be successful:
1.The negligent party owed a duty of care to the victim.
2.There was a breach of the duty of care.
3.Causation (the negligent caused the injury/loss).
4.Damage or injury occurred.

What is England law elements of Tort of Negligence ?

Negligence simply refers to failure to use reasonable care. In common law negligence is explained as the action taken that
contradicts with what an ordinary reasonable member from a given community would act in that same community. It's doping something that a prudent person wouldn't do. It is the legal cause of damage if it directly, naturally and continuously contributes in causing that damage. It is thus taken that were it not for negligence, then the damage
would not have occurred. On the other hand, a tort is any wrongful act except breach of trust or contract resulting in injury to another individual's property and reputation for which the injured individual qualifies to be compensated.

There are three elements in the tort of negligence; duty of care, breach of the duty and damages. Duty of care means that
any single person must always take reasonable care so that he can avoid omissions and acts that he can foresee reasonably as likely to result to injury to his neighbor. In negligence law, a neighbor is that person who is directly and closely
affected by one's act such that one is supposed to have him/her in contemplation to be affected when directing the mind to the omissions and acts in question. Standard of care must be proved by deciding whether the defendant in question owed

the plaintiff a standard of care, the level of standard of care that the defendant owed the plaintiff and lastly, by determining whether another reasonable person in the same field like the defendant would do the same.

Breaching of the standard of care must be proved by checking how likely the injury was and how it can be regarded, injury gravity (whether the plaintiff at all engaged in a dangerous activity) and efforts that may be required in
order to remove injury risk (whether the defendant failed to act reasonably). Damages caused by the defendant must have resulted through the breach of duty of care and that this was not remote.

(11) What is the difference between tort and contract ?

The difference between tort and contract is easy to identify if you understand the concept of each clearly. In fact, the terms Tort and Contract are not uncommon or ambiguous terms. Indeed, we have heard their use occasionally and thus
have a fair idea as to what they mean. However, in order to understand the difference between tort and contract, we must first pay attention to the definitions of each term separately.

The concept of Tort is an important subject in civil law. Indeed, civil courts hear and determine many cases involving Torts. The term Tort is derived from the Latin word 'Tortus,' which is translated to mean "wrong" or "civil wrong." It is similar to the concept of a crime in that it involves some form of wrongdoing inflicted on another person. However, unlike a crime, a Tort is more personal. Thus, while a crime constitutes a wrongful act caused not only to a person but to the entire society as a whole, a Tort constitutes a wrongful act caused only to a person. It is thus a private wrong. Torts typically encompass wrongful acts in the form of harm or injury caused to a person or their property. The party that has suffered harm or injury will file a civil action in court against the person who inflicted the harm. If the court finds that a Tort has been committed, the court will typically order the defendant to pay compensation or provide other relief to the injured party. This compensation is generally known as the remedy of Damages.

Examples of Torts include occupier's liability, nuisance, economic Torts, negligence, defamation, or product liability. The Tort of negligence revolves around the concept of the duty of care owed by one person to another. Failure to exercise this duty of care to another in certain situations will result in the Tort of negligence. An example of such an instance is when a person drives recklessly and causes harm to a pedestrian.

Torts are categorized into Intentional Torts (a person had substantial knowledge that his/her actions would result in harm),strict Liability Torts (Torts which focus only on the physical aspect of the wrongful act), and Negligent Torts. When a person commits a Tort, the court will not look at the Tort but at the harm or injury suffered by the victim as a result of that Tort. Keep in mind that breach of contract does not fall within the definition of a Tort.

- Difference Between Tort and Contract

A tort is a wrong that is personal in nature.

A Contract is a familiar concept to all of us. In simple terms, it refers to an agreement between two or more parties, which is enforceable by law. Formally, however, it is defined as an agreement between two or more parties, who intend to create legal obligations, to perform some work or service. Contracts may be oral or written, although today it is most often in written form. The defining feature of a Contract is that it is not just an agreement to perform some work or service, but that work or service is typically performed in return for a valuable consideration. Thus, consideration is a vital element in a Contract.

Consideration is usually in the form of a payment. In addition to Consideration, a Contract must typically contain several other elements in order to be valid and recognised as a Contract in law. Thus, there must be an offer and an acceptance of that offer, the parties must have capacity to contract, and the subject matter of the Contract must be legal. Contracts may take various forms such as Unilateral Contracts or Bilateral Contracts. Like in the case of a Tort, a breach of one or more of the terms of the Contract or the entire contract itself may result in the remedy of Damages been awarded. Thus, contract is a agreement between two or more parties that is enforceable by law and the difference between Tort and Contract is simple: a Tort constitutes a civil wrong while a Contract refers to an agreement between two or more parties.

In conclusion, the principle difference is between tort and contract. It may include as below:

· A Tort refers to a civil wrong. It is a private wrong in that it constitutes a wrongful act in the form of a harm or injury caused to a person or their property. Torts are categorized into Intentional Torts, Strict Liability Torts, and Negligent Torts.

· A Contract refers to an oral or written agreement between two or more parties, who intend to create legal obligations, to perform some work or service in return for a valuable consideration, which is usually in the form of a payment.

● What is the concept of Tort and Contract difference?

When a person commits a Tort, the court will not look at the Tort but at the harm or injury suffered by the victim as a result of that Tort.

The court will typically order the defendant to pay compensation or provide other relief to the injured party. An examples of Torts include occupier's liability, nuisance, economic Torts, negligence, defamation or product liability.

A Contract has an offer and an acceptance of that offer and the parties involved must have capacity to contract. A breach of Contract by either party may result in awarding the remedy of Damages. An example of a Contract is an agreement between Company A to provide a security service to Company B in return for a valuable consideration paid by Company B to Company A.

(12) What is the difference between a tort and a criminal act?

When it comes to the difference between a tort and a criminal act, the two can be especially difficult to distinguish. Here are the basics:

· Legally speaking, a tort occurs when one's negligence directly causes damage to a person or property.

· A crime is defined as a wrongdoing against society.

● Tort law means

Tort law is the area that determines whether or not a person should be held legally responsible for someone' injuries or damaged property. This area of law also governs the types of damages an injured person is able to collect, such as medical expenses or lost wages. Tort disputes are settled in civil court settings with one party seeking compensation from another.

There are several types of torts, and each covers a wide array of cases. They include:

· Negligence. Negligence is the most common type of tort. These take place when a person acts without due care and, as a result, unintentionally injures someone.

· Strict Liability. In strict cases (for example, animal attacks or defective products) one party is always held liable regardless of circumstances – even if the injury was caused unintentionally.

· Intentional Torts. Intentional torts occur when an individual intentionally causes harm to another, such as battery or defamation. Confusingly, intentional torts often involve criminal activity and are therefore often confused with criminal wrongdoing. However, if the injured party chooses to sue for compensation, the case then also becomes a tort case.

● What are mean of Crimes law?

Crimes are different from torts in that those who have committed a crime have acted against society rather than just an individual person. Crimes are actions that a state or the federal government has deemed illegal.

● Can Crimes Also Be Torts?

As mentioned above, crimes can also be torts in some cases.

For example, let's say Logan and Chris find themselves arguing. Logan punches Chris angrily and breaks Chris's nose as
a result. Logan is then accused of battery – a criminal charge – because it is illegal to physically assault another person in such a way. However, Chris also decides to sue Logan for the medical costs he has accrued due to his broken nose. As soon as Chris sues for his own personal damages, the case also becomes a tort. Logan may have to repay his debts to both society (in the criminal case) and Chris (in the tort case).

- Workers Compensation on contract law protection

When You're Injured

- How to File a Work Injury Claim
- Reporting a Work-Related Injury or Condition
- Workers' Compensation Overview

Obtaining Treatment & Benefits

- Workers' Compensation for Law Enforcement Officers
- Reasons Why Temporary Disability Benefits Can Be Terminated in Your Workers' compensation Case
- Workers' Compensation Case Timeline

Differences between Crimes and Torts

A crime is a wrong arising from a violation of a public duty. A tort is a wrong arising from the
violation of a private duty. Again, however, a crime can also constitute a tort. For example, assault is
a tort, but it is also a crime. A person who is assaulted may bring criminal charges against the
assailant and may also sue the assailant for damages under

tort law. An employee's theft of his employer's property that was entrusted to the employee constitutes the crime of embezzlement as well as the tort of conversion. The police may prosecute a crime, and the offender is imprisoned, but this does not compensate the injured party; to obtain compensation the injured party will need to
bring a claim in tort law.

(13) What does Economic torts mean?

Economic torts are defined as torts that have inflicted pure financial loss on someone. A primary example of an economic tort is 'passing off' in the course of business, whereby an individual or business attempts to pass off their goods as the goods of another – relying on the substantial goodwill associated with the original product or goods. A claim can be made for damages to compensate for the economic loss suffered.

Other claims in tort include tortious claims also include nuisance, occupiers liability, defamation, trespass and breach of confidence.

Remedies in tort,there are two key remedies available for claimants:

- Damages
- Injunction

What do Damages mean?

Damages provides financial compensation to the claimant for their losses. Damages can be broken down into the following subcategories:

- Nominal: where a tort has been committed but the victim has suffered no loss.
- Contemptuous: where the claimant is successful but the court considers that it should not have been brought and

was without merit.
A very small or derisory amount of damages may be ordered in such cases.

· General: to compensate for non economic damages such as pain and suffering and emotional distress.

· Special: the claimant must plead these damages as part of the action and prove that the damage was in fact suffered. For instance,
damage to property and medical expenses.

· Aggravated damages: if the court decides that the tort was committed in a malicious manner, ie. to harm the claimant's character or
question his dignity, then aggravated damages may be awarded.

· Exemplary or punitive damages: these may be awarded when the court finds that the action committed by the defendant is so serious that an example needs to be made of them.

Injunctions means that in some cases, it may be appropriate to apply to the court for an injunction. An injunction is a court order prohibiting or requiring a certain course of action to be taken. This can be in addition to a damages claim.

What do defences to tort actions mean?

The following are defences to tort actions:

· Vicarious liability

· Contributory negligence

· Volenti non fit injuria

Vicarious liability means that where a tort was committed by an employee while undertaking his or her duties of employment, i.e. there was a close and direct connection with the harmful act committed by the employee and what they were employed to do, the employee can deny liability and claim that the employer was vicariously liable.

Contributory negligence means that this is a partial defence used whereby the claimant is accused of acting in a careless manner at the relevant time, and therefore contributed to the injuries or loss which they have suffered.

(14) Reasons need tort law ?

A tort is any civil wrong for which the law provides a remedy. Torts provide compensation for injuries to persons and property caused by the fault of another. There have always been concerns about whether there should be restrictions on tort law because of disagreements about who should bear the financial burden for an injury and what injuries should be compensable. Powerful lobbies of doctors, hospitals, insurance companies and product manufacturers are always appealing to Legislatures to limit the ability of the public to obtain compensation for violations of tort law. Consumers who are injured by defective products, victims of sexual harassment, drunk drivers, and many other civil wrongs are always under attack with their legal ability to be compensated for their injuries.

The purpose of tort law is to restore someone who has been injured as a result of the wrong of another to the condition they were prior to the injury by awarding them monetary damages which will pay for medical expenses, lost wages and compensate for physical
and mental pain and suffering as a result of their injuries.

Beyond this, however, is the role that tort law plays in punishing the misconduct of corporations and individuals who cause harm to others through negligent misconduct.

The existence of our tort law makes it more expensive for corporations and other potential defendants to be negligent or have negligent policies. The fear of being in a lawsuit and having a jury determine what damages have been incurred by a negligent corporation or individual, causes those potential defendants to be more careful and to have policies to prevent injury.

Without tort law, a corporation or individual may chose not to be more careful particularly when being careful requires the expenditure of money. Trial lawyers pursuing tort claims often uncover documents and cover-ups that can have deadly consequences to unprotected individuals. Lawyers who handle cases involving personal injury do so on a contingent fee basis meaning they charge a percentage of recovery rather than an hourly fee which enables individuals with lesser incomes to bring suit against the most powerful individuals and corporations.

● Why the Tort System is Important ?

The tort system gives average people a way to influence powerful businesses and institutions and change their dangerous practices and policies.

· For years, people reported instances of clergy abuse to church officials. However, it was not until lawsuits were filed that church hierarchies began to institute procedures to punish offenders and protect parishioners.

· As a result of lawsuits brought by patients' families, nursing home policies and procedures have been changed to better protect elderly patients.

· After individuals successfully sued companies, many re-designed their products, improved warnings,and in some cases, withdrew dangerous products from the marketplace. The tort system deters companies from putting profits ahead of safety.

· The prospect of paying damages provides the financial incentive for companies to ensure safety and refrain from harmful conduct, thereby preventing injuries in the first place.

· Corporate Risk Managers have reported that the threat of tort liability helps them motivate companies to improve product safety.

· Liability concerns have helped spur the manufacture of safer consumer products, such as flame retardant pajamas and cars with rear-seat shoulder belts and improved fuel tank design.

The tort system helps limit the government's role.

· Without the tort system to police and deter business misconduct, government probably would have to assume a greater role in protecting the public from negligent and unscrupulous business conduct.

(15) Tort law sample cases question

Architect and engineering firm owed duties of care to Provincial to exercise due diligence in their work on project contract liability in tort case:

To satisfy the court that compensation should be made, the plaintiff in a tort action must substantiate that:

1. the defendant owed the plaintiff a duty of care,
2. the defendant breached that duty by his or her conduct, and
3. the defendant's conduct caused the injury to the plaintiff.

Both the architect and engineering firm owed duties of care to Provincial to exercise due diligence in their work on the project. The architect breached his contractually-owed duty of care by ignoring the engineer's recommendation and not doing a detailed enough soils test for building construction. The engineering firm breached its implicit engineering duty of care by submitting a soils report based on inadequate data. The combination of these actions indeed caused financial injury to Provincial. These combined mean that both the engineering firm and the architect satisfy the requirements for tort liability and so should be required to compensate Provincial for any damages that resulted as concurrent tortfeasors.

(Optional: Mention a specific case.) This case is very similar to the 1979 decision by British Columbia Court of Appeal: Corporation of District of Surrey v. Carrol-Hatch et al.: An architect designed a police station which was built and later required extensive structural changes due to soil problems. Engineers working for the architect recommended doing deep soil tests, but the architect rejected the request. The engineers then submitted a soils report to the owner based on two shallow soil tests. Result: engineers 40% liable, architect 60% liable to the owner for structural changes. As such, the result for this case will likely be similar.

Principles of tort law,

"To satisfy the court that compensation should be made, the plaintiff in a tort action must substantiate that:

1. the defendant owed the plaintiff a duty of care,
2. the defendant breached that duty by his or her conduct, and
3. the defendant's conduct caused the injury to the plaintiff."

The standard of care engineers have a duty to uphold is "to use reasonable care and skill of engineers of ordinary experience."

In this case, dependent on the terms and conditions of the contract, CRUDDI may or may not be liable to OILI for the costs of replacing the air conditioning unit and perhaps even lost production as a result. If this is the case, then CRUDDI could take action against MESSI for an amount equal to the damages; otherwise, OILI could commense action against MESSI directly.

MESSI will likely be found liable under tort for the air conditioning replacement and lost productivity as a result of the

original unit's inadequacy because

1) they as engineers had a duty to "use reasonable care and skill of engineers of ordinary experience" in designing the air conditioning unit,

2) they breached this duty by designing a wholely inadequate system for the purpose it was intended, and

3) this breach caused financial injury to OILI .

Answer to this contract law case

Yes, I do think the owner would be successful in a tort claim against the engineer.For liability in tort to exist, three things must be present

1. "the defendant owed the plaintiff a duty of care,

2. the defendant breached that duty by his or her conduct, and

3. the defendant's conduct caused the injury to the plaintiff."

In fact, this is an actual case (Law Text section 4.4): 1983 by Ontario Supreme Court: Unit Farm Concrete Products Ltd. v. Eckerlea Acres Ltd. et al.; Canama Contracting Ltd. v. Huffman et al.

Contractor engaged by owner to construct barn to be placed over a manure pit.

The contractor succeeded with action against an engineer of the dept. of Agriculture, because the contractor relied on advice of the engineer, a friend of the contractor, in confirming that his (ultimately very faulty) design was sufficient. Interestingly, the engineer was not a consulting engineer, nor was he employed to review the plans; he just gave them a quick look as a friend and told the contractor “Good set of plans. I like the detail. Wish I could spend that amount of time on each project. Keep up the good work.” The engineer didn’t know he was being consulted, but the court pointed out that, when “being held to account for negligence, it is not what we subjectively feel or think but what our conduct objectively makes the other person believe we feel or think.” Each found 50% responsible for damages.Contractor appealed this case to the Court of Appeals, which held the engineer 75% responsible and the contractor 25% responsible.

As such, the result in this case will be the same due to precedent. For liability in tort to exist, three things must be present .

1. "the defendant owed the plaintiff a duty of care,
2. the defendant breached that duty by his or her conduct, and
3. the defendant’s conduct caused the injury to the plaintiff."

In this case, SPECS owed ACE a duty of care to design a procedure which conformed with the standard practice at the time, simply by virtue of being engineers, but also by virtue of their contractual relationship. Phil Scooper had a similar duty to KING through contract to act according to the generally accepted practice of his trade, and KING had a duty through contract to ensure that services they hire as part of their contract with ACE are carried out correctly. Both parties breached their duties by their conduct, and the combination of these breaches caused extra costs and a four-week delay to ACE. As such, Phil Scooper and SPECS are concurrent tortfeasors to ACE (although Scooper is technically a tortfeasor to KING and KING to ACE), and likely will be found liable to compensate ACE for the direct extra costs and the indirect ones associated with a four-week delay.

QUEEN will likely be found vicariously liable for Scooper in line with the fundamental principle of tort law being "to compensate victims"
and not "to punish the negligent."

Principles of tort law:
1. the defendant owed the plaintiff a duty of care,
2. the defendant breached that duty by his or her conduct, and
3. the defendant's conduct caused the injury to the plaintiff.

In this case, the new engineer owed Mammoth a duty of care owed by all engineers, but specifically in his capacity as advisor on the matter of whether or not to use the substitute fill material. The new engineer acted negligently by approving a material as safe without doing the necessary analysis to determine whether it was so; breaching a duty of care. Finally, this conduct caused financial injury to Mammoth. As such, Mammoth is entitled to claim damages necessary to replace the material and cover any costs incurred by the associated delay from the engineering firm (or perhaps its insurance company). The firm (or insurance company) would be vicariously liable for the new engineer in line with the fact that the fundamental principle of tort law is to compensate the victims, rather than punish the negligent.

For liability in tort, the three requirements are:
1. "the defendant owed the plaintiff a duty of care,
2. the defendant breached that duty by his or her conduct, and
3. the defendant's conduct caused the injury to the plaintiff."

In this case, the engineering firm (specifically, the recent engineering graduate who designed the sprinkler system and the P.Eng who reviewed it) owed National a duty of care. In not familiarizing him/herself with the NFPA codes at least to the point of determining the sprinkler coverage limits, the engineering graduate breached this duty of care, UNLESS he/she specifically pointed out to the P.Eng his/her only very brief review of the NFPA. Certainly though, the P.Eng breached his/her duty of care in only briefly reviewing the work of the recent engineering graduate and finding it satisfactory.

Finally, this combination of the conduct by the engineering graduate and the P.Eng caused substantially more fire damage to the plaintiff than would have been caused had they not acted negligently (as was substantiated by the consulting engineer's expert opinion "the fire should have been quickly extinguished and would not have spread to any great extent").

According to the Regulations under The Professional Engineers Act of Ontario, negligence is "an act or omission in the carrying out of the work of a practitioner that constitutes a failure to maintain the standards that a reasonable and prudent practitioner would maintain in the circumstances." This is exactly what the engineering graduate did (though ignorantly) in designing the sprinkler system, and also what the P.Eng did in finding the design satisfactory.

Certainly, given the satisfaction of the requirements of tort law, National will be compensated for all excess fire damage and the funds necessary to repair the faulty sprinkler system design. The question remaining is "from whom should this compensation originate?" The necessary principle of tort law to answer this question is “The fundamental purpose of tort law is to compensate victims of torts.”

Though perhaps the most directly at fault in this case, the recent engineering graduate is likely not in a good financial position to compensate National, and so will not likely be assigned liability.

The essential principles of tort law are;

(a) a duty of care,

(b) a breach of that duty,

(c) resulting damage, excess costs or injury as a result of the breach.

The architect had an overall duty of care to ensure a satisfactory system and the mechanical engineering firm to ensure design calculations were correct. These duties were breached and dollars were required to replace the air conditioning system. The engineering firm is vicariously liable with the employee engineer who prepared the design and made significant errors. The engineering firm and the architect are jointly liable i.e. concurrent tortfeasors.

The failure occurred within two years which is within the limitation period for a claim in tort.

The total excess costs to meet completion must be sustained by the architect and the mechanical engineering firm. These costs include the $2,000,000.00 to complete the project and also the costs of delays to the developer/ owner. A likely outcome of the matter is the mechanical firm would be 70% responsible and the architect 30% responsible.

The liabilities of the soils experts Acme Underground, are to see the work is finished so payment by the municipality is limited to the original amount agreed. Since the extra cost is $350,000.00, then this is the basic liability. Other costs, e.g. fees of Subsurface Wizards would also fall to Acme. If the possibility of these liabilities were not included in the various contracts, it would be a suit in tort. A tort case has three elements:

a) a duty of care,
b) a breach of that duty,
c) resulting damages or excess costs to an injured party.

In this case, the soils experts, Acme Underground (a) failed to exercise the care that could reasonably be expected of competent practitioners and (b) made significant errors. The municipality is entitled to a contribution/retribution for the (c) unplanned difficulty. Assuming there is no privity of contract between the owner and the soils experts, the suit would be in tort, unless the engineer's contracts enable action on behalf of the owner.

The likely outcome is all excess costs would be assessed to Acme Underground, an amount of $350,000.00. Sharp did extra work as well which he might claim against Acme.

Even though the municipality's budget was $1,800,000.00 and there was a resultant total cost of $1,650,000.00 plus $350,000.00, the municipality should still only pay the contract price of $1,650,000.00.

Principles of tort law:
"To satisfy the court that compensation should be made, the plaintiff in a tort action must substantiate that:
1. the defendant owed the plaintiff a duty of care,
2. the defendant breached that duty by his or her conduct, and
3. the defendant's conduct caused the injury to the plaintiff."

In this case, the architect breached his contractually-owed duty of care by ignoring the engineer's recommendation and not doing a detailed enough soils test for building construction. The engineering firm breached its implicit engineering duty of care by submitting a soils report based on inadequate data. The combination of these actions indeed caused financial injury to Provincial: as such, the architect and engineer could be found concurrent tortfeasors.

(16) What Are The 4 Elements Of Tort Law?

Every civil lawsuit except for contractual disputes falls under the category of tort law. Essentially, any civil lawsuit is tort law. The premise behind these laws is to provide compensation to victims of wrongdoings. However, not every tort case is successful. So how can you make sure your tort case is successful? For any civil lawsuit to be successful, there need to be four elements of tort law present and proven in court. In this post, we'll outline the four elements of tort law. After reading this post, you'll know where you stand in any potential
tort lawsuit case.

A duty of care must always be present in any tort law claim if it's to be successful. This is basically stating that there is a duty of care on part of the person or the manufacturer of some product that must be upheld. For example, drivers of cars have a duty of care to drive safely and not intoxicated or under the influence of drugs.

Going with the example above, let's say you have Brian who can legally drive in the UK and has his own car. Well, Brian has a certain duty of care that he must adhere to at all times as a responsible driver and not engage in behaviours that could endanger others. Examples of this duty of care he has are not getting behind the wheel drunk or affected by drugs. This is a duty of care Brian has that is enforceable by law so he must adhere to it at all times.

- Breaching Duty Of Care

We've established in the previous section that Brian has a certain duty of care and legal responsibility he must adhere to.

If he were to breach this care, whether it's intentional or unintentional, he could be liable for a tort. For example, if he was to drive his car drunk and then run a red light, which resulted in an accident then he would be found guilty of breaching his duty of care. Therefore, he'd be liable for a tort.

- Causation Which Results In Suffering

This part is crucial for a tort case because there needs to be the action that has caused suffering to the victim. In the absence of the cause, there is no case for a tort.

A key aspect of causation that a court will explore is whether or not the victim's injuries would have occurred had the offender not committed the specific action that resulted in the injury to the victim.

Let's return to the case of Brian being drunk and running a red light. If while running a red light, he crashed into another car,which resulted in the other driver becoming permanently brain damaged from the crash, then this would be sufficient causation for a tort.

- Damage Or Injury to above case?

It is difficult to decide damage or injury to this case, because without the damage or injury sustained then there is no basis for a tort lawsuit. Let's roll with the case of Brian above. The other driver he crashed into must have sustained some sort of injury from his negligent actions.
If there is an absence of physical, mental, or emotional damage then Brian cannot be liable for a tort.

It's also important that these damages are proven for there to be a legitimate case. To prove mental and emotional damages, you'd need to get expert proof from professionals in this area. To prove physical damages, advice from medical professionals would be required.

What Happens If A Tort Is Proved ?

If all the four elements of tort law above are present then a tort has been committed. In this circumstance, there is going to be a court case where either damages or an injunction occurs. There are various damages that can be awarded in this instance such as full compensation where the victim must be fully compensated monetarily for his/her suffering.

However, there are various subcategories of damages that can be awarded like nominal damages, special damages, aggravated damages, and more. Victims will pursue any of the damages most applicable to their specific situation in order to get the compensation they deserve. Ultimately, it's up to the court to decide what damages will be awarded.

What does negligence mean in tort law ?

Negligence refers to failure to use reasonable care. In common law negligence is explained as the action taken that contradicts with what an ordinary reasonable member from a given community would act in that same community. It's doping something that a prudent person wouldn't do. It is the legal cause of damage if it directly, naturally and continuously contributes in causing that damage.

It is thus taken that were it not for negligence, then the damage would not have occurred. On the other hand, a tort is any wrongful act except breach of trust or contract resulting in injury to another individual's property and reputation for which the injured individual qualifies to be compensated. There are three elements in the tort of negligence; duty of care, breach of the duty and damages.

Duty of care means that any single person must always take reasonable care so that he can avoid omissions and acts that he can foresee reasonably as likely to result to injury to his neighbor. In negligence law, a neighbor is that person who is directly and closely affected by one's act such that one is supposed to have him/her in contemplation to be affected when directing the mind to the omissions and acts in question. Standard of care must be proved by deciding whether the defendant in question owed the plaintiff a standard of care, the level of standard of care that the defendant owed the plaintiff and lastly, by determining whether another reasonable person in the same field like the defendant would do the same. Breaching of the standard of care must be proved by

checking how likely the injury was and how it can be regarded, injury gravity (whether the plaintiff at all engaged in a dangerous activity) and efforts that may be required in order to remove injury risk (whether the defendant failed to act reasonably).

Damages caused by the defendant must have resulted through the breach of duty of care and that this was not remote.

For hospital doctor's a duty of care to patient case example:

In this case in question, B (patient) was examined by A (doctor) since he had a chest problem. A had asked B all the relevant questions just like any other doctor in this field would have done. But after being discharged B died due to a heart attack. It is the prescription that B's wife believes caused the death of her husband. Applying the tort of negligence,

B who is the claimant in this case must satisfy three elements as required by the clinical negligence law. A owed B a duty of care since he is a medical professional. In order for the court to rule in the favor of B (claimant), she must show that A breached the duty of care owed to her husband by treating him negligently. This should include a sound proof that A did not establish a reasonable standard of skill and care. This would call for detailed medical evidence in our case. In the end, a loss/damage (death) caused must be shown that its causative agent was due to A's breach of duty.

For manufacturer's duty of care to consumer case example:

Taking as an example, Donoghue v Stevenson is a case where the tort of negligence developed. It was in 1929 when Donoghue (plaintiff) bought a ginger beer manufactured by Stevenson (defendant). This ginger beer was in an opaque bottle that could not allow one to see its contents clearly. Donoghue consumed some of the beer but as she poured the remaining beer into her glass,

decomposed remains of a snail
were seen in the glass. She had gastro-enteritis and nervous shock which she claimed were due to the snail remains in the beer. Just like in our case of A and B, the defendant (Stevenson) owes a duty of care to the plaintiff (Donoghue). The main issue in deciding this case was on establishing whether Stevenson owed Donoghue a duty of care. Lord Atkin said decisively that Donoghue had to show that the damages
caused to her were due to the breach of duty owed to her by Stevenson in taking reasonable care to avoid it. The court by using previous cases like Heaven vs. Pender asserted that negligence comes due to a moral wrongdoing where the offender is obliged to pay.

Additionally, a person must take reasonable care to escape all acts and omissions that one can reasonably foresee that they can injure ones neighbor. They thus ruled that this may be a grave law defect where consumers cannot sue manufacturers for negligently mixing a drink with poison. By stating that the manufacturer must have the foreseeability of the effects on actions taken on the neighbors (consumers).

In case of A and B, it shows that there is medication negligence according to UK law.
The defendant after examining the plaintiff and asking all the relevant questions, he did not fully exercise his duty of care.

The medication that killed B can only be taken as lack of exercising the required standard of care for a professional of A's caliber. A doctor in the same position would have been expected to give medications to B that coincided with the problem that he had. According to UK law, medical negligence occurs where an individual who is trained in the

medical profession fails to fulfill his
duties of care to his patients in a standard manner.

B's wife must that have to proof just like it was proved in above case by the court whether there is duty of care owed to her husband by A.

A doctor has to take all the actions towards his patients to ensure that whatever he does will not cause any injury to them. Comprehensive medical evidence is required here to show that B died because of medication negligence of A. This may be hard for her to proof since the heart attack may have been caused by other health problems. Three pre-conditions formulated in Caparo v Dickman for imposition of duty of
care (sufficient proximity between parties, it should be just, fair, and reasonable in imposing the duty of care in the circumstances and foreseeabilty of harm) must come into play in A vs. B so that B can claim compensation. It's evident that sufficient proximity between A and B exists.

The prescription given to B may however not make A to foresee any harm because all the questions he asked and the examinations he carried out on B had convinced him that he was supposed to give B that prescription. However, despite this, a doctor is supposed to act just like all others would do in the same profession. It is the duty of A to exercise standard of care after examining B and asking all the questions to make sure that diagnoses is not performed to the detriment of the patient (B).

For Tort of negligence of auditor case example:

Tort of negligence is also applied in Caparo v Dickman (1990) HL. In this case, the auditors of the company had prepared the accounts that however could not show that the company had been making losses. On seeing the accounts of the company, Caparo thought that since this company was not making any losses as per the auditors' accounts, it was advisable for him to buy shares in the same company. This company was however making losses. Caparo (plaintiff) thus alleged that it was through negligence that he was owed a duty of care.

A previous case, Sutherland Shire Council v Heyman (1995) was referred to and it was declared that the law must come up with novel categories in negligence in accordance with the already established categories. It was rejected for extension of duty of care to indefinable people or class of persons who are owed. In this case, it was ruled that there was no duty of care owed.

The auditors won this case since there was no case that could hold them to have a duty of care to the plaintiff.

To the auditors, establishing whether there was a duty of care required the court to determine whether the loss to the plaintiff was foreseeable.

This was not possible for the auditors. Again, there was no established proximity between the two parties to the case. Thus it was not just, fair or even reasonable for imposition of duty of care.

In Perrett v Collins (1998) CA, a plane built by Collins crashed and Perrett, a passenger was injured. This was a light aircraft that had been severally inspected at various stages. After its completion, Mr. Usherwood who was one of the inspectors approved it. Authorities had given

certification that the plane was airworthy. This shows that both the inspector and the certifying authority were liable due to negligence as they had certified this experimental plane fit to be flown. The duty of care was thus to be extended to any passenger in it. The public is supposed to be protected from any injury through mindful operation of the plane system. A passenger in such a plane has to be compensated as this is negligent operation. By doing this, they have imposed a duty of care that is owed to the public by Collins.

For a duty of case to doctor and injuries patient case example:

Duty of care was also established in Watson v BBBC (1999) CA (Goodey, 2007). The defendant, British Boxing Board of Control could not provide sufficient medication. Watson, a boxer suffered brain damage as he was injured on the ring. Evidence provided showed that those brain injuries would have been prevented if there was better medication at ringside. Here, the sports body owed all participants a duty of care. Injury in boxing competitions is always foreseeable. Proximity was also created by the licensing system.

By looking at all the circumstances it was fair, reasonable and just in imposing duty of care. Duty of care alleged was not avoiding to cause personal injury but to have reasonable care that ensures that injuries caused are properly treated. These two cases seem to concur with the case of A and B. By being a doctor who is professionally trained;

it means that A is a registered doctor who is expected to perform his duties just like other doctors in the profession. He owes a duty of care to all his patients. By being a registered doctor, it establishes proximity between A and B. Drugs administered to a patient are not guaranteed

that they will always produce the expected results. Injury is thus foreseeable. Looking at all the circumstances in A vs. B, it was fair, just and reasonable to impose a duty of care. These two cases helps us to use the three pre-conditions of establishing that a duty of care exists as

alleged by B's wife.

A doctor must exercise a standard duty of care to his patients. B's wife is claiming that her husband died due to the faulty medication that was given. After asking questions and examining B, A gave medical treatment that B's wife thinks was the cause of her husband's death. A in his profession is supposed to carry out his activities just like others would in the same field. His actions were supposed to be reasonable. It's all irrelevant for the defendant to claim that the medical treatment he gave B was the right one. His perception or what he thinks was okay is irrelevant since expectations are; he must act reasonably. It doesn't matter here if A considers his conduct fine; the standard is what would be expected of a reasonable person in medical profession. Standard of care in negligence doesn't result to absolute duty in prevention of injury.

Duty instead amounts to what the reasonable person is supposed to do to prevent injury from occurring. Reasonable test would be used here so that it can be decided what would be the reasonable behavior of A. In this case, the court would consider several factors. Special characteristics of A (defendant), special characteristics of B (claimant), how far it was practical to prevent this risk and magnitude of this risk. For A, he is a doctor and thus he has special skills (profession). Law expects a doctor to exhibit competency standards just like another doctor would do. This amounts to reasonable behavior. This same standard would apply even if the defendant was inexperienced or experienced.

For negligent act to learner driver and driver teacher case example:

In Nettleship v. Weston (1971), it was ruled that a learner driver was judged against standards of competent driver. Weston's inexperience could not be used as an excuse that her driving was below expected standard from a competent driver. Weston was thus considered negligent as her negligent act resulted in damage. In the case of A vs. B, A would be held negligent as he has acted below the expected competence level.

When considering the claimant (B), the court would have expected A (reasonable person) to look into incapacity or special characteristics which
would have increased the injury. Magnitude of the risk would also be considered. This incorporates chance of the damage occurring and then the seriousness of the resultant damage. This may be illustrated in Vaughan vs. Menlove case where Vaughan built a haystack while Menlove who was a neighbor occupied a cottage that was near this haystack. Vaughan was given advice that his haystack could catch fire as it was not properly ventilated. It later caught fire. It was ruled that a reasonable person could have taken the necessary precautions.

The court in the case of A v B will thus consider how far it was practical to prevent the risk. In medical negligence, it is stated that a doctor cannot be held negligent in cases where he provides proof that what his
did is an act that has been agreed by the relevant body in the medical profession. A doctor can defend compensation to the
claimant successfully if he shows that the reputable body of doctors would act in the same way as he did. In A v B, A had
asked B all the relevant questions which another doctor in the same position would have done. Additionally, A had examined B properly as he was complaining of chest pains.

It clearly shows that medical treatment or prescription was given to B after doing all what any other reputable doctor would have done. It's clear that A as a medical expert had an opinion that was reasonable. The medication that he gave B was after weighing up the benefits and the risks involved. It's through this that he made his logical conclusion to give that particular treatment. This is just like in the case of Bolam v Friern Hospital Management Committee 1957.

In this case, a patient was treated for psychiatric problems yet he had an electric shock. The relaxant drugs administered led to broken bones. In the profession, there were doctors who felt that these drugs are not supposed to be given while others felt that they should.

Since some doctors believed that these drugs administration was okay, the court ruled in favor of the doctor as this was a practice that was in accordance with other professionals.

For doctor's duty of care to patient case example:

Another example is Bolitho vs. Hackney Health Authority 1997 where a two year old was admitted to hospital with breathing difficulties but was not seen by the doctor. He alter died of a heart attack. His mother claimed that he should have been seen by a doctor and incubated but failure to this resulted to his death. An expert witness from the doctor was produced which showed that incubation would

not have been the correct treatment for Bolitho while the claimant (Bolitho's mother) also came with a witness who said that incubation would have been the best treatment. Here the court ruled in favor of the doctor by stating that the opinion of the medical experts was reasonable and they had weighed up the risks and benefits.

Their conclusion was thus logical. It was thus declared that the doctor was negligent. The same case would apply in A vs. B. A has the capacity to produce evidence that all the examinations that he did and the questions asked were the relevant things any medical expert would have used. A thus weighed the risks, benefits and had a logical conclusion when he gave that particular medication to B. A was not liable for breach or it's totally possible to declare that there was breach of duty.

Death occurred in this case. B's wife must however prove that death was caused by breach of duty. The omission/negligence of A must be shown to be the cause the death of B. The UK law does not make defendants liable and infinitum. Instead, tests are applied to determine what injury was caused by the defendant. The major test that would be applied here is 'but for' test. It simply means that the court will ask itself whether the claimant would not have suffered the injury 'but for' the omission/negligence by the defendant. There is no exact connection between the death of B since his death through a heart attack could have been due to other health problems. B's wife must in addition prove that the death caused was not remote from A's breach. A would only be liable for those injuries he would have caused B and he could have reasonably foreseen them at breach time.

The law of neglience claimant to succeed, the court must be satisfied that the defendant in question owed him a duty of care, that there was breach of duty by the defendant and finally the claimant's damages were as a result of the breach.

Thus in our case, its well established that A as a doctor owed B a duty of care, but breach of the doctors duty could not be established though death (damage/injury) occurred.

Since all the elements in tort law are not served, then B's wife does not have a sufficient legal standing to take this case to court.

(16)Difference Between Tort Law and Criminal Law

We know that they both involve an act of wrongdoing. Tort means wrong. A crime, on the other hand, also denotes a wrong, a very serious one. Despite the fact that both recognise and declare certain acts as wrongful and therefore unacceptable, there is a difference. It lies in the types of wrongful acts that fall within the purview of each body of law.

What is Tort Law?

A Tort refers to a civil wrong. This means that Tort Law is dealt with in a civil proceeding. Tort Law encompasses situations in which harm has been caused to a person or property. Typically, the person who suffered harm initiates an action in a civil court against the person who caused the harm. Further, in a case involving Tort Law, the person who suffered injury sues the party at faul to in order to obtain relief or compensation for the injury. Compensation under Tort Law is typically awarded in the form of damages. Damages can include damages for loss of earnings, property, pain or suffering, financial or medical expenses.

Think of Tort Law a party seeks compensation of a financial nature for the loss he/she suffered. Examples of Torts include negligence, defamation, liability for defects in products, nuisance or economic torts. Negligence revolves around the duty of care and the failure to exercise a duty of care in a particular instance; for example, causing a motor accident.

It has three categories of Torts: Intentional torts, such as when a person had fair knowledge that his/her action would cause the harm, strict liability torts, which by their very definition exclude the degree of care exercised by the guilty party and instead focus solely on the physical aspect of the action such as the harm caused. There are also negligent torts, which involve the unreasonableness of a guilty party's actions.

What is Criminal Law?

Criminal Law encompasses the world of crime. It is defined as a wrong arising from the violation of a public duty. Think of Criminal Law as dealing with wrongful acts that affect society or the public collectively; in the sense that it disrupts the peace and order of society. This is in contrast to Tort Law, which deals specifically with wrongful acts that affect an individual personally.

Criminal Law is a body of law that regulates the conduct of society and ensures the protection of citizens by punishing those who do not act in accordance with such law. The crimes of murder, arson, rape, robbery and burglary are crimes that affect the society as a whole. For example, if there are a series of murders committed by one person, more commonly referred to as serial killing, then, the safety of society is at risk. Crimes falling within the purview of Criminal Law are dealt with in a criminal proceeding. Criminal law deals with instances in which an individual commits a crime against societal rules. For example, robbing a bank is considered criminal activity. Civil law, on the other hand, takes over when a dispute exists between private individuals. Case in point, one major area of civil law involves divorce and other family law proceedings.

In some cases, an individual may choose to sue another for injuries or damages. This is called tort law, and it falls under the umbrella of civil law.

Although tort law is considered part of "civil law," many other areas of civil law exist as well. These include divorce and family law, contract disputes, wills and property disputes. Any dispute between private individuals, as stated above, typically fall under civil law jurisdiction.

Tort law is the largest area of civil law. The purpose of tort law is to determine whether or not an individual should be held legally accountable for the injury of another person. Tort law is also used to determine whether or not an individual should be compensated for his or her injuries and how much money is owed. For example, if someone slips and falls in a workplace accident, tort law is responsible for determining if the employer is liable for the individual's injuries and the amount of workers' compensation due.

3 Types of Tort

There are three prominent areas of tort law:

•Intentional tort. An intentional tort is when an individual purposefully engages in conduct that causes an injury or damages. For example, defamation and fraud each fall under intentional tort.

•Negligence. Negligence takes place when one person fails to do their duty to prevent injury or accident, leading to damages. Negligence includes slip and falls and car accidents. It's the most common type of tort.

•Strict liability. Sometimes absolute liability applies to a tort case. This occurs when one party is solely responsible for damages or injury. These include cases of defective products and animal attacks.

When compared to tort law, penalties are more severe in criminal law. Though tort law aims at providing compensation to the victim; punitive damages are also awarded in special cases. Almost all jurisdictions have enacted laws for protecting the citizens from wrongdoings, which are classified as crimes and torts. Both criminal law and tort law are intended to punish the offenders and deter others in society from indulging in such wrongdoings. If both crimes and torts are wrongful acts that are against the interests of society, then why are they treated differently? In fact, crimes and torts are different in various ways. In order to find out the difference between torts and crimes, you have to understand their meanings.

Every person has a legal duty to respect others' legal right and not to infringe such rights. Defamation is an example of a tort in which the reputation of a person is damaged by another. So, tort is a private wrong that affects the person or property of an individual. It is a civil wrong for which the aggrieved party may sue the wrongdoer for damages, according to tort law. A crime is an action or omission that constitutes an offense that may be prosecuted by the state and is punishable by law. It is a wrongful act committed in violation of a law prohibiting it, or omitted in violation of a law ordering it. In short, certain acts are classified by the state as crimes, and committing such acts gives rise to criminal liability. Robbery is an example of a crime. So, a crime is a public wrong, which is considered as a wrongdoing against society as a whole. It is a criminal wrong, for which the wrongdoer is punished by the state, according to criminal law. Given below is a comparison of torts and crimes, and the laws regarding these wrongdoings.

In concluson, both criminal law and tort law are used for taking corrective action against wrongdoers. As torts are wrongdoings against individuals, tort law is aimed at providing redress to aggrieved parties and deterring people from committing torts. The main purpose is to compensate the victim for the harm he/she suffered as well as crimes are considered as wrongdoings against the state or society as a whole. Certain acts are classified by the state as crimes, and such acts are forbidden by law; as they threaten public safety and welfare. Though a crime may have created an immediate victim(s), the state is considered as the ultimate victim; because a criminal (like a robber) can be dangerous for any person in society if he is let loose. So, the main purpose of criminal law is to protect society from crimes.Civil law is any law that is not criminal. Tort law is a subset of that — the law of non-criminal interpersonal injury (personal or economic). It does not include such civil issues as probate, family, civil rights, property law, or bankruptcy, among others.

CHAPTER II

Crime law basic elements questions

(1) Criminal Law definition

A body of rules and statutes that defines conduct prohibited by the government because it threatens and harms public safety and welfare and that establishes punishment to be imposed for the commission of such acts. The term criminal law generally refers to substantive criminal laws. Substantive criminal laws define crimes and may establish punishments. In contrast, Criminal Procedure describes the process through which the criminal laws are enforced. For example, the law prohibiting murder is a substantive criminal law. The manner in which government enforces this substantive law—through the gathering of evidence and prosecution—is generally considered a procedural matter.

Crimes are usually categorized on their nature and the maximum punishment that can be imposed. It involves serious misconduct that is punishable by death or by imprisonment for more than one year. Most state criminal laws subdivide into different classes with varying degrees of punishment. Crimes that do not amount to violations. It is misconduct for which the law prescribes punishment of no more than one year in prison. Lesser offenses, such as traffic and parking infractions, are often called violations and are considered a part of criminal law.

Congress has the power to define and punish crimes whenever it is necessary and proper to do so, in order to accomplish and safeguard the goals of government and of society in general. State legislatures have the exclusive and inherent power to pass a law prohibiting and punishing any act, provided that the law does not contravene the provisions of the U.S. or state constitution. When classifying conduct as criminal, state legislatures must ensure that the classification bears some reasonable relation to the welfare and safety of society. Municipalities may make designated behavior illegal insofar as the power to do so has been delegated to them by the state legislature.

Laws passed by Congress or a state must define crimes with certainty. A citizen and the courts must have a clear understanding of a criminal law's requirements and prohibitions. The elements of a criminal law must be stated explicitly, and the statute must embody some reasonably discoverable standards of guilt. If the language of a statute does not plainly show what the legislature intended to prohibit and punish.

In deciding whether a statute is sufficiently certain and plain, the court must evaluate it from the standpoint of a person of ordinary intelligence who might be subject to its terms. A statute that fails to give such a person fair notice that the particular conduct is forbidden is indefinite and therefore void. Courts will not hold a person criminally responsible for conduct that could not reasonably be understood to be illegal.

A criminal statute does not lapse by failure of authorities to prosecute violations of it. If a statute is expressly repealed by the legislature, but some of its provisions are at the same time re-enacted, the re-enacted provisions continue in force without interruption. If a penal statute is repealed without a saving clause, which would provide that the statute continues in effect for crimes that were committed prior to its repeal, violations committed prior to its repeal cannot be prosecuted or punished after its repeal.

The same principles govern pending criminal proceedings. The punishment that is provided under a repealed statute without a saving clause cannot be enforced, nor can the proceeding be prosecuted further, even if the accused pleads guilty. A court cannot inflict punishment under a statute that no longer exists. If a relevant statute is repealed while an appeal of a conviction is pending, the conviction must be set aside if there is no saving clause. However, once a final judgment of conviction is handed down on appeal, a subsequent repeal of the statute upon which the conviction is based does not require reversal of the judgment.

Generally, two elements are required in order to find a person guilty of a crime: an overt criminal act and criminal intent. The requirement of an Overt Act is fulfilled when the defendant purposely, knowingly, or recklessly does something prohibited by law. An act is purposeful when a person holds a conscious objective to engage in certain conduct or to cause a particular result. To act knowingly means to do so voluntarily and deliberately, and not owing to mistake or some other innocent reason. An act is reckless when a person knows of an unjustifiable risk and consciously disregards it.

Ordinarily, a person cannot be convicted of a crime unless he or she is aware of all the facts that make his or her conduct criminal. However, if a person fails to be aware of a substantial and unjustifiable risk, an act or omission involving that risk may constitute negligent conduct that leads to criminal charges. Negligence gives rise to criminal charges only if the defendant took a very unreasonable risk by acting or failing to act.

(2) What does criminal intent mean?

Criminal intent must be formed before the act, and it must unite with the act. It need not exist for any given length of time before the act; the intent and the act can be as instantaneous as simultaneous or successive thoughts. A jury may be permitted to infer criminal intent from facts that would lead a reasonable person to believe that it existed. For example, the intent to commit Burglary may be inferred from the accused's possession of tools for picking locks.

Criminal intent may also be presumed from the commission of the act. For example, the intent to commit murder may be demonstrated by the particular voluntary movement that caused the death, such as the pointing and shooting of a firearm. A defendant may rebut this presumption by introducing evidence showing a lack of criminal intent. In the preceding example, if the murder defendant reasonably believed that the firearm was actually a toy, evidence showing that belief might rebut the presumption that death was intended.

Proof of general criminal intent is required for the conviction of most crimes. The intent element is usually fulfilled if the defendant was generally aware that he or she was very likely committing a crime. This means that the prosecution need not prove that the defendant was aware of all of the elements constituting the crime. For example, in a prosecution for the possession of more than a certain amount of a controlled substance, it is not necessary to prove that the defendant knew the precise quantity. Other examples of general-intent crimes are Battery, rape, Kidnapping, and False Imprisonment.

Some crimes require a Specific Intent. Where specific intent is an element of a crime, it must be proved by the prosecution as an independent fact. For example, Robbery is the taking of property from another's presence by force or threat of force. The intent element is fulfilled only by evidence showing that the defendant specifically intended to steal the property. Unlike general intent, specific intent may not be inferred from the commission of the unlawful act. Examples of specific-intent crimes are solicitation, attempt, conspiracy, first-degree premeditated murder, assault, robbery, burglary, forgery, false pretense.

Most criminal laws require that the specified crime be committed with knowledge of the act's criminality and with criminal intent. However, some statutes make an act criminal regardless of intent. When a statute is silent as to intent, knowledge of criminality and criminal intent need not be proved. Such statutes are called Strict Liability laws. Examples are laws forbidding the sale of alcohol to minors, and Statutory Rape laws.

The doctrine of transferred intent is another nuance of criminal intent. Transferred intent occurs where one intends the harm that is actually caused, but the injury occurs to a different victim or object. To illustrate, the law allows prosecution where the defendant intends to burn one house but actually burns another instead. The concept of transferred intent applies to Homicide, battery.

For murder criminal behavior example. It is not necessary to prove that the defendant intended to kill the victim. For example, a death resulting from arson will give rise to a murder charge even though the defendant intentionally set the structure on fire without intending to kill a human being. Furthermore, the underlying crime need not have been the direct cause of the death. In the arson example, the victim need not die of burns; a fatal heart attack will trigger a charge of felony murder. In most jurisdictions, a death resulting from first-degree murder, usually include arson, robbery, burglary, rape, and kidnapping.

(3) What does malice criminal behavior mean?

Malice is a state of mind that compels a person to deliberately cause unjustifiable injury to another person. At Common Law, murder was the unlawful killing of one human being by another with malice aforethought, or a predetermination to kill without legal justification or excuse. Most jurisdictions have omitted malice from statutes, in favor of less-nebulous terms to describe intent, such as purpose and knowing.

Criminal law has retained malice as an element in criminal prosecutions. malice is an essential element of first- and second-degree murder. According to the Supreme Judicial Court of malice is a mental state that "includes any unexcused intent to kill, to do grievous bodily harm, or to do an act creating a plain and strong likelihood that death or grievous harm will follow.

(4) What does criminal law motives mean?

Motives are the causes or reasons that induce a person to form the intent to commit a crime. They are not the same as intent. Rather, they explains why the person acted to violate the law. For example, knowledge that one will receive insurance funds upon the death of another may be a motive for murder, and sudden financial difficulty may be motive for burglary.

Proof of a motive is not required for the conviction of a crime. The existence of a motive is immaterial to the matter of guilt when that guilt is clearly established. However, when guilt is not clearly established, the presence of a motive might help to establish it. If a prosecution is based entirely on Circumstantial Evidence, the presence of a motive might be persuasive in establishing guilt; likewise, the absence of a motive might support a finding of innocence.

(5) What does Defenses mean?

Defenses Negating Criminal Capacity To be held responsible for a crime, a person must understand the nature and consequences of his or her unlawful conduct. Under certain circumstances, a person who commits a crime lacks the legal capacity to be held responsible for the act.Examples of legal incapacity are infancy, incompetence, and intoxication.

In legal view point, children are not criminally responsible for their actions until they are old enough to understand the difference between right and wrong and the nature of their actions. Children under the age of seven are conclusively presumed to lack the capacity to commit a crime. Between the ages of seven and 14, children are presumed to be incapable of committing a crime. However, this presumption is not conclusive; it can be rebutted by the prosecution through the admission of evidence that the child knew that what he or she was doing was wrong. Anyone over the age of 14 is presumed to be capable of committing a crime, but this presumption can be rebutted by proof of either mental or physical incapacity. So, children do not need to defence to responsible for a crime behavior in criminal view point.

(6) What does a criminal lawyer do?

Criminal lawyer needs to advises clients about the potential consequences of a course of action.

A criminal lawyer helps their client understand criminal laws. They also help the client understand how their actions may or may not violate a criminal law. A defense attorney might help their client understand whether a proposed course of action is a crime. An attorney for the state might help law enforcement officers understand best practices for enforcing the law.

A criminal lawyer also need to help their client present their case or present a defense. A prosecutor or district attorney presents evidence and pursues prosecution of cases on behalf of the unit of government that they represent. They make decisions about whether to extend a plea offer. They present the evidence on behalf of the state at trial. A defense attorney helps their client present a defense. A defense attorney gathers evidence for their client. They evaluate the case in order to determine viable defenses. If they need to file pretrial motions, they make sure they file the motions in the right way.

In any countries, citizens have constitutional rights. No unit of government can pass a law that violates a person's right to be free from an unreasonable search and seizure. Law enforcement also can't keep a person in jail for an indefinite period of time. Criminal attorneys must know how the constitution and criminal law intersect. They must be aware of constitutional implications of law as they go about their work and advocate for their clients as necessary in order to protect and defend their constitutional rights.

Why does criminal lawyer need tp practise criminal law ?

A criminal law practice requires diverse skills and a capacity for memorization. It's also exciting. For lawyers who like frequent court appearances and the occasional appearance on television, criminal law is a good fit. Criminal lawyers must be comfortable in high pressure situations. They also must be able to think on their feet.

There often isn't time to look something up or seek a second opinion when they must act in a matter of seconds to move to admit evidence or make an objection.

Criminal law is a good fit for lawyers who choose to focus on state laws in a small geographic region can expect to have multiple court hearings a week. They can expect to conduct trials and other contested hearings. Lawyers who focus on crime also have the academic challenge of building a case. They review police reports and interview witnesses. They examine possible defenses and determine whether or not they apply to the case. Being an effective criminal lawyer requires a well rounded mix of academic skills and oral advocacy. Criminal lawyers also benefit from having a high capacity for rote memorization. A criminal lawyer needs have good writing and speaking skill. Criminal lawyers can't rely on speaking or writing alone. A criminal lawyer must write clearly in order to properly file motions and help the court understand nuanced issues of law. They must also have the trial advocacy skills to conduct complex trials. Whether a lawyer advocates on behalf of the state or for an accused, they must also have the interpersonal skills to interact with the other side and the jury.

(7) What are stages in a criminal law case ?

In first stage, a criminal case starts with an arrest or the filing of formal charges. Ultimately, it's up to an attorney for the government to decide to charge a person with a crime. While the police can make an initial arrest, a person doesn't formally face charges until the state's attorney files them.

In second stage, an arraignment is the first court appearance. A judge or magistrate formally reads the accused person the details of the charges they're facing.

They set a bond amount and conditions of bond. In rare and serious cases, they may order law enforcement to hold the person without bond until resolution of the case.

In thord stage, the defense has time and power to gather information about the case. The defense can serve a discovery demand that requires the state's attorney to produce evidence about the case. The state's attorney always has an ethical obligation to provide the defense with evidence that might be favorable to their defense.

In final stage, if the parties reach a resolution, the case may not go to trial. The state might agree to dismiss the charges, they might agree to dismiss the charges with conditions, or they might reach a plea resolution. If the parties can't resolve the case, a judge or jury may hear the evidence at a formal trial. If the jury finds the defendant not guilty, the case ends. If they find the defendant guilty, the case proceeds to sentencing.

(8) Felony and misdemeanor offenses mean

Crimes are classified as felony offenses and misdemeanor offenses. Typically, a crime is a felony if the maximum possible penalty is more than one year in jail. A felony usually brings the possibility of going to a state prison rather than a local jail. A misdemeanor is a crime that carries a maximum penalty of less than one year in jail.

Some states have low-level misdemeanors that don't carry the possibility of jail time. For example, in Michigan, a minor who drives with a blood alcohol content is guilty of a misdemeanor that's punishable by only a fine and community service. Each state may have unique classifications for a few types of offenses. For example, for certain felony offenses in Texas, offenders face only the possibility of confinement in a state jail for not less than 180 days or more than two years.

(9) What makes a law a crime?

Criminal law is the area of law that relates to prohibited conduct in society. When government leaders take steps to ban certain actions, they create crimes. Criminal law is the area of law that involves enforcing criminal law as well as defending against allegations of violations of criminal law.

The purpose of outlawing conduct is to protect society. Law makers typically pass a law with the belief that it's for the public good. Criminal laws must be applied evenly to everyone. Lawmakers can't make a law that targets only one person. The purposes of punishing criminal offenders include retribution, deterring certain behaviors, preventing additional offenses and rehabilitation of offenders.

How to cause a criminal behavior?

An act isn't a crime just because government officials prohibit the behavior. Instead, a behavior is a crime because of the penalties that are attached to a violation. In the case of a crime, a person's freedom is usually on the line. Each crime carries a maximum penalty. That penalty is the most amount of time that a person can spend in jail if they're convicted of the offense. A criminal offense often has other penalties such as a fine, probation and placing a record of the offense on a person's public, criminal history. However, the distinguishing characteristic of criminal law is that a person who commits a criminal offense might spend time in jail or prison.

(10) What are elements of a crime?

Crimes can be broken down into elements, which the prosecution must prove beyond a reasonable doubt. Criminal elements are set forth in criminal statutes, or cases in jurisdictions that allow for common-law crimes. With exceptions, every crime has at least three elements:

a criminal act, also called actus reus; a criminal intent, also called mens rea; and concurrence of the two. The term conduct is often used to reflect the criminal act and intent elements.

If a crime does require a bad result, the prosecution must also prove the additional elements of causation and harm. Another requirement of some crimes is attendant circumstances. Attendant circumstances are specified factors that must be present when the crime is committed. These could include the crime's methodology, location or setting, and victim characteristics, among others.

In general case, the prosecution has to prove the elements of criminal act, criminal intent, and concurrence for attempted murder. The prosecution does not have to prove causation or that Conrad was harmed because attempt crimes, including attempted murder, do not have a bad result requirement. The criminal statute, or case in jurisdictions that allow common-law crimes, describes the criminal act element. One requirement of criminal act is that the defendant perform it voluntarily. In other words, the defendant must control the act.

Status as a Criminal Act

Generally, a defendant's status in society is not a criminal act. Status is who the defendant is, not what the defendant does. Similar to punishment for an involuntary act, when the government punishes an individual for status, it is essentially targeting that individual for circumstances that are outside his or her control. This punishment may be cruel and unusual pursuant to the Eighth Amendment if it is disproportionate to the defendant's behavior.

(11) What is criminal intent ?

Criminal intent is a necessary component of a

"conventional" crime and involves a conscious decision on the part of one party to injure or deprive another. It is one of three categories of "mens rea," the basis for the establishment of guilt in a criminal case. There are multiple shades of criminal intent that may be applied in situations ranging from outright premeditation to spontaneous action.

It is possible to establish criminal intent even when a crime is not premeditated. Individuals who commit a crime spontaneously may still understand that their actions will cause harm to another party and contravene existing criminal law. In other words, an individual that takes or withholds action with the knowledge that such behavior will lead to the commission of a crime can be said to possess criminal intent.

While criminal intent is a necessary component of mens rea in virtually every modern legal system, its particulars may vary between jurisdictions. There often exists a distinction between "basic intent" and "specific intent."
Since it requires a lighter burden of proof, the former is used more often to establish criminal intent.

For instance, an individual who strikes a pedestrian crossing the street in a marked crosswalk can be said to have exhibited "basic intent" whether or not they intended to cause the pedestrian harm. There are two reasons for this.
First, the driver may have ignored state and local law requiring vehicles to yield to pedestrians in crosswalks. Absent such laws, the driver either failed to pay close attention to the road ahead or assumed that the pedestrian would be able to avoid their oncoming vehicle. In either case, the driver abdicated their legal responsibility to take reasonable precautions to ensure the safety of others on the

road.

"Specific intent" is invoked less frequently and often applies to cases in which the accused intends to commit a crime but has not yet done so. It may be used to justify preventive detentions associated with terrorism, treason or sabotage. For instance, an individual who has communicated his intent to assassinate an official may be judged to exhibit specific intent on the basis of his or her pronouncements.

Criminal intent may be further categorized as either "direct" or "oblique." Defined as a desire to commit a specific act in the expectation that it will result in a specific outcome, the former may be used to prove premeditation. For instance, an individual who purchases a firearm and uses it in a mugging exhibits direct intent to threaten another with deadly force.

By contrast, "oblique" intent may be used to establish guilt in cases that involve unintended consequences. An individual who undertakes a specific action with the knowledge that it may cause certain consequences can be said to have oblique intent. For instance, an individual who injures someones by firing a gun into the air near a crowd may be held responsible for that injury despite a lack of direct intent to cause harm.

Criminal intent means the intent to do something wrong or forbidden by law.

Intent refers to the state of mind accompanying an act especially a forbidden act. It is the outline of the mental pattern which is necessary to do the crime. At times criminal intent is used in the sense of mens rea-the mental element requisite for guilt of the offense charged.

Example of a case law on criminal intent. Where a person intends to kill or injure someone, but in the course of attempting to commit the crime accidentally injures or kills a third party, the defendant's criminal intent will be transferred to the third party. Under this doctrine called the Felony murder doctrine, the felonious intent involved by underlying felony may be transferred to supply intent to kill necessary to characterize the homicide as murder

(12) Why does society need criminal law?

Society needs criminal law, it may incldue these reasons: The criminal law regulates how we as individuals deal with each other and how companies and businesses, deal with us and indeed how the government local and national deals with us.The criminal law is in place to ensure that we as individuals comply with a set of rules that if we break the state will punish us.

The aim is to ensure that we do not take the law into our own hands and seek our own justice by harming the person we think has harmed us.

The purpose is for us to be protected from the actions of others by ensuring that those others are aware of an effective set of sanctions that are there to deter them from committing a crime and harming us as individuals.

It is to deter people from committing crime, however whether the punishment actually deters people from committing crime is debatable particularly in cases of sexual abuse. In those circumstances the criminal law is in place to ensure that the victims of crime are empowered to report things that have caused them harm in the past and to ensure that individuals who presents a risk to society, for example by virtue of their position of power, or other circumstances, are prevented from harming anyone in the future . If these defendants are placed in prison the reason is for public protection and often sentences are put in place to ensure this. If on the other hand people require simple punishment but not rehabilitation the deprivation of liberty, then that is the function of a prison sentence as well.

The probation service offer the possibility of rehabilitation within the community and it is often the case that such community-based options are more successful and certainly cheaper than prison based option. Public opinion in general is considered by the public as a soft option. The reality is that it is not. Defendants offending behaviour is challenged and ongoing supervision in the community is in reality a significant change to the way a person lives their life. However the perception of the public has been difficult to challenge even though the statistics show the potential for a lower reconviction rate.

The emphasis in terms of punishment has significantly changed in the past 10 years in that the victims of crime often dictate, (to an extent) the punishment and level of seriousness of the court should take into consideration. Victim impact statements are read out in court.

It is very difficult to explain to victims and family that there are punishments that are more effective than Prison. Prison sentences are getting longer and longer and the prison population is growing faster than the beds are available.

At some point the emphasis on imprisonment will have to change, simply because the financial resources are no longer available. Imprisonment, although necessary, is a very expensive way of dealing with offenders. Is it time for a rethink perhaps.? The reasons for the criminal law being so important is wide and various, the object of a good system of criminal law in my opinion is this:-

"to protect and serve the community as a whole by dealing fairly with people who cause us harm or loss, for the benefit of the community as a whole"

(13) What is Criminal Justice Reform?

Criminal justice reform is working to end the number of prisoners in the justice system through both litigation and advocacy. By fighting for nationwide reform at a variety of government levels, the nation can right wrongs before the problem becomes worse.

While no criminal justice system is entirely perfect, neither is that of the United States. Reform aims to fix these errors, and there are a number of organizations involved in the movement in various ways, including:

•Reducing harsh prison sentences
•Changing the drug sentencing policy surrounding the war on drugs
•Decriminalizing certain laws, including drug policies
•Prioritizing rehabilitation of offenders, especially juvenile offenders
•Altering policies surrounding food assistance programs and voting rights for previous offenders
•Changing minimum sentencing laws

(14) What are the three consequences , when the police arrest the defendant?

When the police arrest someone (the defendant), they take him or her to jail.

Then, 1 of 3 things happens:

• The defendant is released if the prosecutor (usually the district attorney or the city attorney) decides not to file charges; or

• The defendant posts bail (also called a "bond") or is released based on a promise to appear in court at a later date for arraignment. If either of these happen, the district attorney or police tell the defendant when to come to court for arraignment; or

• The defendant stays in jail. Law enforcement officers transport the defendant to the court

(15) How a Case Starts ?

The first step, usually, the police cite or arrest someone and write a report. This report summarizes the events leading up to the arrest or citation and provides witnesses' names and other relevant information. Defendants generally do NOT have a right to get a copy of the arrest report, but their lawyers do. The reason for this is to protect the identity of witnesses. This is another reason why it is important that a defendant charged with a misdemeanor or felony have a lawyer to represent him or her.

The second step, theprosecutor then decides whether to file charges and, if so, what charges to file. The prosecutor decides whether to charge the crime as a felony or a misdemeanor. The prosecutor can file charges on all of the crimes for which the police arrested the defendant or can decide to file fewer charges or more charges than were included in the arrest report.

The final step, because defendants have a right to a speedy trial, the prosecutor must generally file charges within 48 hours of the arrest when the defendant is in custody (in jail). Weekends, court holidays, and mandatory court closure days do not count against the 48 hours. Also, the deadline for arraignment depends on what time of the day you were arrested, so talk to a lawyer to find out exactly when the prosecutor's deadline to file charges is. All above steps are any cases are caused before all these steps are needed to passed.

(16) What does Trial mean?

Trial may need to cause that defendants in criminal cases (other than infractions) have the right to have a jury of their peers decide their guilt or innocence. Therefore, before trial, defendants need to decide whether to have a jury trial (where the jury decides if the defendant is guilty or not) or a court trial (where the judge decides). Usually, defendants choose to have a jury trial because they want a jury of their peers to hear the evidence and decide their guilt. But sometimes there may be circumstances where a defense attorney will recommend a court trial without a jury.

Everyone accused of a crime is legally presumed to be innocent until they are convicted, either by being proved guilty at a trial or by pleading guilty before trial. This means that it is the prosecutor who has to convince the jury that the defendant is guilty and must provide proof of guilt beyond a reasonable doubt. The defendant has the right to remain silent and that silence cannot be used against him or her.

(17) How to setting a Trial Date?

For a jury trial for a misdemeanor case: The law says how soon a defendant charged with a misdemeanor must be brought to trial. If the defendant is in custody at the arraignment, the trial must start within 30 days of arraignment or plea, whichever is later. If the defendant is not in custody at the arraignment, the trial must start within 45 days of arraignment or plea, whichever is later.

The defendant can "waive" (give up) the right to a speedy trial. This means the defendant agrees to have the trial after the required deadline (also known as "waiving time"). But even if the defendant waives time, the law says the trial must start within 10 days after the trial date is set. It is very important for defendants to get advice from an attorney before they waive time. The prosecutor must file the Information within 15 days of the date the defendant was "held to answer" at the preliminary hearing. The trial must start within 60 days of the arraignment on the Information. The defendant can "waive" (give up) the right to a speedy trial. This means he or she agrees to have the trial after the 60-day period (also known as "waiving time"). It is very important for defendants to get advice from an attorney before they "waive time."

(18) What Happens at Trial?

Before the trial starts, the lawyers choose a jury. The process for choosing a jury is called "voir dire." During this process the attorneys on both sides ask questions of the potential jurors to make sure the jurors will be fair and impartial.Before the lawyers present evidence and witnesses, both sides have the right to give an opening statement about the case. During the trial, lawyers present evidence through witnesses who testify about what they saw or know. After all the evidence is presented, the lawyers give their closing arguments.Finally, the jury decides if the defendant is guilty or not guilty. The jury must find the defendant guilty beyond a reasonable doubt.

(19) What will occur after the trial the appeal process ?

If you are found guilty after a trial, you have the right to an appeal process. There are many reasons for an appeal of a criminal case, but appeals are also very difficult, so talk to a lawyer to make sure you know what is best for you.

There are also important deadlines that apply to appeals. If you miss the deadline, your appeal will most likely be dismissed.

For misdemeanor cases, you must file a Notice of Appeal (Misdemeanor) within 30 days of the date of the judgment or order. For felony cases, you must file a Notice of Appeal — Felony (Defendant) within 60 days of the date of the judgment or order.

Keep in mind that the appeal is not a new trial. The appellate court can review the evidence (testimony and exhibits) presented at your trial to see if the trial court made a legal error in how the testimony or exhibits were received. The appellate court does NOT decide the facts of the case as the judge or jury in the trial court does.

You can only appeal if:

1. You say there was not enough evidence in your trial to justify the verdict or judgment; and/or
2. You say there were mistakes of law during or before the trial that hurt your case.

If you say there was not enough evidence in your trial to justify the judgment, the appellate court will review the record and decide if there was substantial evidence to support the judgment. If you say mistakes of law were made, the appellate court will hold a hearing to listen to both parties. Then they will decide if there was any irregularity or mistake that prejudiced (hurt) your case. In addition to appealing after a trial, there are other situations when you can file an appeal, like appealing the validity of a plea or probation violations. Talk to your lawyer to learn more about your options to appeal.

• If you are appealing a misdemeanor conviction, you can appeal to the appellate division of the superior court. Read the Information on Appeal Procedures for Misdemeanors if you want to appeal a guilty conviction in a misdemeanor case.

• If you are appealing a felony conviction, you can appeal to the Court of Appeal in your appellate district

• If you are appealing an infraction case, read the Information on Appeal Procedures.

(20) Why do we need a criminal justice system?

The basic formation of the criminal justice system comprises of law enforcement, courts and correction. However, the pivotal role of the Criminal Justice System is to deter and investigate crime. A criminal justice system is the law and order of a society. Therefore, a strong, impartial and accountable criminal justice system, which protects the human rights of accused and victims, rich and poor, young and old alike, is the cornerstone of a just and impartial society.

The criminal justice system implemented decades ago to control the lower classes of society. Throughout the years, this system had improved to accommodate different classes, those of different status or groups of society. This implementation extends equality across all the society. The criminal justice system is a crucial part of our society and we know that comprehensive, effective, and nondiscriminatory implementation of criminal justice system powers is essential to ending violence, both for freeing individual and for ending the worldwide epidemic of violence against one another in this human race.

Why do our societies need for a criminal justice system ?

The public knows that the police cannot prevent every crime, nor apprehend every criminal. However, they expect a criminal justice system, which is reliable, effective, and respected. It must deal with cases efficiently; fight crime in each state and each town in this country. Thus, the society needs criminal justices system to protect, to deter and to prevent crime. Obviously, the idea of having a system is to ensure fairness and equality throughout a social setting.

The criminal justice system is a system that requires management by different organisations accordingly. This system consists of the police, courts and corrections. Each organisation takes responsibility of and facilitates different parts of the system to set rules or to procedures laid down by the government according to the needs of the society.

The criminal justice system is designed for a coherent administrative system for offenders. Without the threat of a punishment for wrong doing, the crime level in a society would be high. This threat that comprises of a functioning criminal justice system is a healthy threat as it brings about social order. The trauma of going through a high and complex criminal justice system turns people away from a causative culture to one of wrong doings. Punishments for crimes serve as a deterrent to criminals.

The goals of the previous criminal justice systems were mainly action based (e.g. apprehending offenders, punishing offenders and etc.). In the present era, our criminal justice system seems to be focusing on education for the public regarding crime and rehabilitation of offenders. This method is implemented to deter offenders or prevent crime from spreading. It emphasises on protecting the citizens and maintaining peace and order.

(21) Why does some one feel to need a criminal defense attorney legal service?

Why does some one want a criminal defense attorney legal service? It may include these reasons:

For property buyer case, when one property buyer needs to buy any property. The property firm company must help him to find one property lawyer to assist them to write one property contract agreement between the property firm and the property buyer in order to achieve the property purchase and sale transaction successfully.

What this means is that legal matters are litigated by putting party A against party B and letting a jury of lay people decide if the complaining party proved its case. On the criminal side, that means that the government has to prove beyond a reasonable doubt that the accused actually committed the crime. The defendant doesn't have to prove a thing...(s)he certainly doesn't have to prove innocence. The, in this tort behavioral complaining situation, the part B may choose to find one lawyer to help him to win the another A party, because the party A sues him and he fears that he will fail to win this sue in court.

Why does part A feel need to find lawyer?

Well think of the consequences of guilt. A person found guilty is branded a convict, and typically deprived of his/her liberty. Those are the direct consequences but there are collateral ones too. For example, a father put in jail won't be at home to support his family. He'll lose any job he had and it'll be all the more difficult to get one when he returns to society. People will brand him a convict and his reputation will forever be affected. Doesn't it make sense to put heavy proof requirements on the government before subjecting an accused to such punishments? So, the government ought need to help the father to find one lawyer to avoid that he needs to put in jail, because if the government feels this father will not done any criminal behavior in this case.

I think that when we give the State power to ruin someone's life and reputation, we should make them earn that power. I think we should keep the government honest. You wanna convict somebody for a crime, you gotta earn that conviction. This line of thinking seems only natural in other aspects of life, doesn't it? Consider politics. When a politician runs un-opposed, doesn't it feel wrong? We want someone to oppose them. After all, a victory in a game without an opponent is hollow.

My point to all of this is that a defense attorney has not only a proper but also an important role in the American justice system. If you take away the defense attorney, you make the process of convicting someone hollow. I, for one, would like to know that when a person goes to jail it's not because of a flawed system but because he actually committed the crime.

BUT HOW CAN YOU DEFEND THE GUILTY?

Truthfully, most people acknowledge what I have stated above. They realize that a meaningful justice system allows both parties a fair fight. But it doesn't matter to them. After all, I just said it takes both sides so why not work for the prosecution? They don't understand how I could represent someone I knew to be guilty. Systemic concerns surely aren't applicable any more right? We're no longer faced with the concern of wrongful conviction, so how can I do it?

First of all, if there's going to be a determination of guilt, would you rather one defense attorney do it or twelve jurors? Maybe I learn in the course of representing my client that he's guilty. Wouldn't you rather the jury be the final voice on that, not me? I don't actually think most people want to see a system where an attorney can abandon his or her client upon learning the status of the client's guilt. And do note, I won't know up front if my client is guilty. I'd never take the police's word for it because of course they think he's guilty. No, my investigation team will do an independent investigation. As a result, it may be several months into the representation before I would know that a client is guilty. You'd really support the idea of abandoning a client halfway through the representation?

Second, representing a client constitutes so much more than just making a guilt or innocence determination. Plenty of defense attorneys negotiate plea deals for their clients each business day. That's right, a defense attorney is advising his or her client to plead guilty. We recognize that many cases will lose at trial because evidence of guilt is very strong. From this point, our job turns to ensuring that our client receives a fair sentence. Thus, when some parties feel that they ought not have crimes, then they will seek lawyers' professional opinions to help them to win the criminal sue case more easily.

(22) What does "criminal procedure" mean ?

When a judge refers to the rules of criminal procedure, he/she is referring the rules which control how a criminal case will be handled. Rules of criminal procedure do not generally define what a violation of the law is, but rather will set out how any given criminal case will be treated as it progresses through the crminal court system. Most criminal cases will begin with an arrest. Before the police can arrest you, they must have probable cause to arrest you. Once you are arrested, you must be arraigned and informed of the charges against you. You have the right to request an attorney at arraignment. The same procedure will apply for all criminal cases.

What are Criminal Procedure Rules ?

The rules of criminal procedure are extremely important to defendants because they are designed to guarantee constitutional due process to those individuals

charged with a crime. Criminal convictions can carry severe consequences, including:
?Paying steep fines and court costs
?Loss of liberty by imprisonment
?Loss of civil liberties, like the right to carry a weapon and the right to vote.

Criminal procedures are designed to make sure that any given defendant receives due process and their constitutional rights are protected. Prior to 1966, very few states had procedures in place to ensure that the constitutional rights of defendants were protected. Because of rules like these, defendants have the right to confront witnesses and the right to remain silent, even during trial.

Criminal Procedure Rule Examples

If a criminal procedure is not followed, you also have the right to challenge the admissibility of the evidence that the state would like to use against you. For example, if the police took a statement from you without providing warnings, the statement could end up being suppressed, or thrown out. Whether your case will be dismissed for a violation of criminal procedures will depend on the nature of the violation and the other evidence against you. Continuing with the same example, if your confession is the only piece of evidence against you, chances are your case will be dismissed if your confession is thrown out. However, if other evidence exists that was legally obtained, the state can proceed with the case against you—they just can't use your confession.

The rules of criminal procedure are in place to protect your rights. However, if you don't exercise them, you could lose valuable protections and remedies. Make sure to tell your attorney if you think your rights were violated and why. Failure to contest a statement taken in violation before or during your trial could result in a waiver. Waiver means that if you didn't tell the trial court your rights were violated, you are banned from bringing it up later on appeal. A lawyer in your area can review your criminal case and make sure that your rights are protected with your state's local rules of criminal procedure.

(23) How Long Does A Criminal Trial Last?

In recent years, many have the idea that criminal trials take a long time due to the high publicity of some cases that seem to have taken forever to be decided. However, most criminal trials do not take nearly as long as the popular media trials would seem to make you think. Usually the entire process from arrest to sentencing takes less than a couple of years to complete.

The first part of any trial process is the arrest phase. This begins the trial process. The arrest phase can occur at anytime within the statue of limitations for a criminal act. This means that as long as the statute of limitations is still in effect this phase of the process can occur whether it has been a few weeks or several years.

The next phase of the trial process is the arraignment phase. This portion of the process usually occurs with the defendant being brought before a judge for a formal hearing informing the defendant of the specific charges being brought against them. This part of the process usually occurs within 48 hours of a defendant's arrest in most jurisdictions. During the arraignment hearing, the judge may also decide whether to release the defendant to return for trial in the case of a misdemeanor charge or may choose to hold the defendant in the local correctional facility in the case of a felony charge. If not, there may be a detention hearing that is held later to determine if the defendant needs to be held or released.

The next phase of the trial is the preliminary hearing phase. This part of the trial process is where the prosecutor shows his or her evidence as to why the court needs to proceed with a trial. The defendant's attorney has the chance to cross-examine any witnesses and to see what exactly the evidence is that the prosecutor is going to use against his or her client. Some prosecutors however will choose to not conduct a preliminary hearing and will move straight into the Grand Jury phase of a felony trial. They may choose this to protect their witnesses and evidence so that this can be brought out in front of the Grand Jury. The preliminary hearing phase of the trial usually takes place 5-6 days after an arraignment.

The next phase of the trial is the motions and hearings phase. This usually takes about 3 months to occur but can last as long as 2 years. During this phase evidence issues are settled and investigations are conducted to determine the allowance or suppression of witnesses. Other motions may be attempted in an effort to get the case dismissed on the grounds that a speedy trial is not being conducted. Overall the motions and hearings have the possibility to delay a case for a good amount of time.

The next stage is the Grand Jury phase. In this phase a group of 16-23 citizens meet to hear the evidence presented by the prosecutor to decide if there is strong enough evidence to support an indictment. Usually the Grand Jury is a part of the prosecutor's office and as such normally hears only one side of the case. The side that they hear is the prosecutor's. The defendant has the right to testify before the Grand Jury and the defense lawyer may get permission for other witnesses to also testify. If things go in the favor of the defendant the Grand Jury may issue an indictment and the trial is over. This phase usually occurs within 6 days of the arraignment if the defendant has not waived this or if this part of the process has not been extended due to issues brought out in earlier parts of the trial. This phase is where the case is argued by the prosecutor and the defendant's attorney in front of a jury and the case is decided in favor of the prosecution or the defense. This portion of the process usually takes about a total of 4 days to 2 weeks. In extremely difficult cases it may take a few months. The Arraignment on Indictment occurs following the Grand Jury phase. This portion of the trial process is similar to the original arraignment but the charges explained will be those that the Grand Jury has issued the indictment for. This portion of the trial usually happens within about 48 hours after the indictment is issued by the Grand Jury.

The next part of the process for a felony case is to move to the motions and hearings phase where the case has evidence, witness, and Constitutional rights issues debated and settled. This part of the trial process can take anywhere from 3 months to a couple of years. Usually though the process is finished in a matter of a few months. Following this, the case moves into the trial phase. This phase of the trial process usually takes from 4 days to 2 weeks. However extremely difficult and complicated cases can take several months. This is where the jury decides the case based on the prosecutor's and defendant's attorney's arguments. Once this is done the case will move forward.

The next phase in both felony and misdemeanor cases is the Pre-Sentencing Investigation phase. This part of the trial process usually takes 1 to 12 months after the conviction to be completed. It can be delayed by up to a year should the judge decide to place the defendant on probation before sentencing. During this time, the evidence is examined and investigated to determine all of the details of the crime and its impact on the victims. Once this has been completed, the trial process moves into the sentencing phase.

The sentencing phase is the final part of the trial process. This usually occurs between 1 and 12 months after conviction. The sentencing is carried out before a judge and then the defendant is notified of the sentence that they are facing. Once this phase has finished the trial process is over unless appeals are filed for higher courts to hear the case.

In all, most cases are finished in less than a couple of years. On the federal side, the defendant is assured that their trial phase should occur within 70 days due to the Speedy Trial Act. An attorney will discuss with the defendant the timing of the case and will explain any delays that may occur. As seen throughout the explanation of this trial process though, all but the most complicated of cases are usually decided and completed in a relatively short matter of time.

CHAPTER III

Contract law questions

(1) Contract law definition

Contact law may define as body of law that governs oral and written agreements associated with exchange of goods and services, money, and properties. It includes topics such as the nature of contractual obligations, limitation of actions, freedom of contract, privity of contract, termination of contract, and covers also agency relationships, commercial paper, and contracts of employment.

Contract may include these elements: It is an agreement with specific terms between two or more persons or entities in which there is a promise to do something in return for a valuable benefit known as consideration. Since the law of contracts is at the heart of most business dealings, it is one of the three or four most significant areas of legal concern and can involve variations on circumstances and complexities.

The existence of a contract requires finding the following factual elements: a) an offer; b) an acceptance of that offer which results in a meeting of the minds; c) a promise to perform; d) a valuable consideration (which can be a promise or payment in some form); e) a time or event when performance must be made (meet commitments); f) terms and conditions for performance, including fulfilling promises; g) performance.

(2) What does a unilateral contract mean?

It is one in which there is a promise to pay or give other consideration in return for actual performance.
For example, I will pay you $700 to fix my car by this week Friday; the performance is fixing the car by that date). A bilateral contract is one in which a promise is exchanged for a promise. (I promise to fix your car by Thursday and you promise to pay $500 on Thursday).

Contracts can be either written or oral, but oral contracts are more difficult to prove and in most jurisdictions the time to sue on the contract is shorter (such as two years for oral compared to four years for written). In some cases a contract can consist of several documents, such as a series of letters, orders, offers and counteroffers. There are a variety of types of contracts: "conditional" on an event occurring; "joint and several," in which several parties make a joint promise to perform, but each is responsible; "implied," in which the courts will determine there is a contract based on the circumstances. Parties can contract to supply all another's requirements, buy all the products made, or enter into an option to renew a contract. The variations are almost limitless. Contracts for illegal purposes are not enforceable at law.

(3) How to cause breach of contract?

In the law of contract a breach of contract occurs when at least one party does not perform his obligations under the contract. A statement or a clear intention that there will be no performance is often known as repudiation. Breach results in an award of damages or specific performance.It means that failing to perform any term of a contract, written or oral, without a legitimate legal excuse. This may include not completing a job, not paying in full or on time, failure to deliver all the goods, substituting inferior or significantly different goods, not providing a bond when required, being late without excuse, or any act which shows the party will not complete the work ("anticipatory breach.") Breach of contract is one of the most common causes of law suits for damages and/or court-ordered "specific performance" of the contract

(4) Specific Performance

It means that an extraordinary equitable remedy that compels a party to execute a contract according to the precise terms agreed upon or to execute it substantially so that, under the circumstances, justice will be done between the parties.Specific performance grants the plaintiff what he actually bargained for in the contract rather than damages (compensation for loss or injury incurred through the unlawful conduct of another) for not receiving it; thus specific performance is an equitable rather than legal remedy. By compelling the parties to perform exactly what they had agreed
to perform, more complete and perfect justice is achieved than by awarding damages for a breach of contract.

Specific performance can be granted only by a court in the exercise of its Equity powers,
subsequent to a determination of whether a valid contract that can be enforced exists and an evaluation of the relief sought.

As a general rule, specific performance is applied in breach of contract actions where monetary damages are inadequate, primarily where the contract involves land or a unique (Personal Property).Damages for the breach of a contract for the sale of ordinary personal property are, in most cases, readily recoverable so that specific performance will not be granted.

An important advantage to this remedy is that, since it is an order of an equity court,

it is supported by the enforcement power of that court. If the defendant refuses to obey that order,

the defendant will be criminal Contempt and even imprisoned. The defendant can also be cited for civil contempt for continuing to refuse to obey the order and until the defendant agrees to obey it.

(5) PRIVITY OF CONTRACT.

The relation which subsists between two contracting parties. For property buying and selling contract example, a lessee has both privity of contract and of estate; and though by an assignment of his lease he may destroy his privity of estate, still the privity of contract remains, and he is liable on his covenant notwithstanding the assignment.

It is the relationship between the parties privy to the contract, i.e. those who are direct parties to it.

Until the passing of the Contracts (Rights of Third Parties) Act 1999, English law did not permit parties not in a relationship of privity to sue on a contract. Thus, a third party benefited by a contract could not sue on it.The effect of the Act has been to substantially relax this rule, although many contracts seeks to exclude the effect of the Act.

(6) Valid Contract

A valid contract means the remedy of specific performance presupposes the existence of a valid contract between the parties to the controversy. The terms of the contract must be definite and certain. This is significant because equity cannot be expected

to enforce either an invalid contract in its terms that equity cannot determine exactly what it must order each party to perform.

It would be unjust for a court to compel the performance of a contract according to ambiguous terms interpreted by the court, since the court might erroneously order what the parties never intended or contemplated.

(7) Consideration means

Consideration is an essential element for the formation of a contract. It may consist of a promise to perform a desired act or a promise to refrain from doing an act that one is legally entitled to do.

In a bilateral contract—an agreement by which both parties exchange mutual promises—each promise is regarded as sufficient consideration for the other. In a unilateral contract, an agreement by which one party makes a promise in exchange for the other's performance, the performance is consideration for the promise, while the promise is consideration

for the performance.

Consideration must have a value that can be objectively determined. A promise, for example, to make a gift or a promise of love or affection is not enforceable because of the subjective nature of the promise.Thus, consideration needs have these elements , they include: 1) payment or money. 2) a vital element in the law of contracts, consideration is a benefit which must be bargained for between the parties, and is the essential reason for a party entering into a contract. Consideration must be of value (at least to the parties), and is exchanged for the performance or promise

of performance by the other party (such performance itself is consideration).

In a contract, one consideration (thing given) is exchanged for another consideration.
Not doing an act (forbearance) can be consideration, such as "I will pay you $1,000 not to build a road next to my fence," So, consideration needs have that which is used to hide the true amount being paid.
Contracts may become unenforceable or rescindable (undone by rescission) for "failure of consideration" when the intended consideration is found to worth less than expected, is damaged or destroyed, or performance is not made properly (as when the mechanic does not make the car run properly). Acts which are illegal or so immoral that they are against established public policy cannot serve as consideration for enforceable contracts. Examples: prostitution, gambling where outlawed, or
inducing someone to breach an agreemen or a promise.

(8) What are the essential characterists of a contract agreement?

To constitute a legal contract, an agreement must have all of the following 5 characteristics:
They may include as below:

A contract must have a legal purpose to be enforceable. For example, Johnny hires Paul to kill Peter. Johny drafts an agreement outlining Paul's responsibilities, namely to acquire a gun and shoot Peter in the head. The agreement also specifies the amount Johnny will pay Paul once Peter is dead. A contract of murder for hire is illegal. If Paul fails to fulfill his obligations under the agreement,
Johnny will have no consideration or payment responsibity against Paul. The agreement Johnny has drafted is unenforceable.

A contract must have Mutual Agreement. All parties to

the contract must have reached a "meeting of the minds." That is, one party must have extended an offer to which the other parties have agreed. For example, Johnny signs a contract with Peter Tree Trimming. The contract outlines the scope of the work Peter will perform on Johnny's property. Johnny and Peter have a mutual agreement regarding the work that will be done.

A contract must have Consideration. Each party to the contract must agree to give up something of value in exchange for a benefit.For example, you hire an independent contractor to repave your driveway. You and the independent contractor sign an agreement in which you promise to pay a sum of money in exchange for the paving work. Both you and the contractor have agreed to give up something of value. You have agreed to pay money, and the contractor has agreed to perform the paving work.

A contact must have Competent Parties. The parties to a contract must be competent. That is, they must be of sound mind,of legal age, and without sign by drugs or alcohol influence. If you enter into a contract with a minor or an insane person, the contract will not be enforced.

A contract must have Genuine Assent. All parties must engage in the agreement freely. A contract may not be enforced if mistakes have been made by one or more parties. Likewise, a contract may be voided if one party has committed fraud or exerted undue influence over another. For example, you sign a contract in which you agree to sell your house to your next-door neighbor for one million. When you signed the contract, your neighbor was pointing a gun at your head. Clearly, you made the agreement under duress, so the contract is not valid, because you sign your house selling agreement from your nexr door neighbor's force behavior.

(9) When does one contract effective date?

The Effective Date or Effectiveness of Agreement clause sets the date when the rights and obligations under the agreement become operational. The Effective Date need not be the same as the execution date. In the absence of an effective date, the terms of the agreement become operational upon execution.Are Contracts That Don't Specify a Date Still Legal?

There are some potential points when you enter into a contract with a vendor or client, especially if you have a contract with no end date_._ While the contract is likely valid, it must detail enough information to outline the agreement and must include the signatures of all parties involved. A contract does not need a date to be valid. Most times, it will simply begin on the day it is signed.

Consideration on one contract effective date, it includes these points as below:

Contract Start Date Considerations, in the absence of a contract expiration date,
it's sometimes confusing to know when a contract begins. In most instances, written contracts that don't specify an effective date begin on the contract signing date. Oral contracts, however, are effective the day that one party accepted the other party's offer because no contract signing date exists. In cases in which the parties involved can't remember the contract signing date then a court will have to determine the effective date by examining other documents related to the agreement, and the actions of each party.

Contract End Date Considerations, when a written agreement lacks a contract expiration date,
and a dispute arises about when the contract ends, a court must examine all aspects of the agreement
to determine when the agreement ended or will end. If you signed a contract to buy laptops from a vendor, for example, a court may determine that the contract expiration date occurred when the supplier delivered the laptops to your business. The court could confirm this by reviewing the receipt of delivery to determine that the contract was completed. In most instances, courts will apply the standard of a "reasonable period of time" based on the terms of the agreement to determine the logical ending of a contract.

Time-Sensitive Contracts, it means that in some instances, two parties may enter into a contract that requires payment on every anniversary of the contract start date. A dispute may arise, however, if there is no written start date. In that instance, a court may default to the day that the parties signed the contract, or in the event of an oral contract, the date an offer was accepted. If neither party is able to remember the date the contract was signed, the court may have to determine the date the first payment was made, and use that date as the anniversary date for each subsequent year.

CHAPTER IV

Competition law question concept and ordinance

- Competition law concept and ordincance

What is Business Law?

Business law is sometimes called mercantile law or commercial law and refers to the laws that govern the dealings between people and commercial matters. There are two distinct areas of business law; regulation of commercial entities through laws of partnership, company, bankruptcy, and agency and the second is regulation of the commercial transactions through the laws of contract. The history of these types of laws dates back several centuries and can be seen in the peace-guilds where members would pledge to stand by each other for protection. A lot of business law involves trying to prevent problems that can hurt the business or cause legal disputes. Business law may include any of the following:

Business law starts with setting up a business. In the eyes of the law, each business is their own legal entity. Starting a new business typically starts with filing the paperwork that makes the business formally exist in the government's eyes. Many types of business entities are similar throughout the country. However, the exact entities that a new business can choose from vary by state. The process to file the paperwork to establish the business also varies from state to state.

Business lawyers help decision makers weigh the pros and cons of each entity when they're starting a business. They help educate the business founders in the law in order to help them choose the entity that's in their best interests. Then, they help them file the paperwork to formally start the business.Business law may include as below:

Employment considerations

Once a business is up and running, they might need employees. Businesses need legal advice to help them understand how to hire and fire employees. They need to know how to handle employee disputes and discipline. Businesses need to know what they need to offer employees in terms of pay and benefits. There are also mandatory payroll taxes and deductions. Business lawyers educate their clients on the rules and best practices for managing employees.

Immigration law

Business law and immigration law often intersect. Businesses may want employees from other countries. They may want international employees on a full-time basis, they may need temporary workers, or they may need to bring in a worker just for a short period of time for a special event. Knowing how to navigate federal immigration laws is an important aspect of business law that helps companies get the manpower they need to succeed.

Sales of consumer goods

Buying and selling isn't as easy as it sounds. There are regulations that govern how companies can make products and how they can sell them. From working conditions in a factory to distribution requirements to price controls, there are all kinds of laws and rules that might regulate how a company makes and sells its products.

One of the most influential documents for business operations is the Uniform Commercial Code. It's a model code that outlines recommendations for commercial transactions. It covers topics such as the statute of frauds, contracts, leases, sales, credit, bulk sales and secured transactions. Business lawyers help their clients identify the laws that a business needs to follow, and they help ensure the company's compliance with the laws.

Contract drafting and negotiations

A lot of business has to do with preparing and negotiating contracts. A contract can be anything from a lease agreement to a purchasing agreement to an agreement with a third-party vendor to sell a product. A lot of contract law comes from common law. Common law isn't written down anywhere. Instead, it's principles of law and rules that have developed through the courts over time. Lawyers in business law have to not only understand the elements of contract law from both statutes and common law, but they must also appreciate the nuances that might impact enforcement of a contract. They must work with their clients in order to skillfully negotiate and draft contracts that work to the client's best interests.

Anti-trust

Most businesses want to control a large share of the market. They want to grow and expand. Companies who want to increase their profits and their market share need to make sure that they go about it in legal ways. Companies that employ deceptive or unfair practices in order to cut out competitors or avoid competition might find themselves the subject of allegations of anti-trust violations. Business attorneys help their clients identify conduct that might amount to anti-trust before the behavior has the chance to create problems for the business.

Intellectual Property

When a business invents a new product, they need to make sure they protect their ability to profit from their invention. Making sure a business gets to exclusively keep and use their own products falls under intellectual property and copyright law. Intellectual property is technical and complicated. Lawyers need to have a scientific background in order to formally practice before the U.S. Patent and Trademark Office. Intellectual property work is critical to helping companies profit from their novel work.Similarly, copyright laws help companies profit from their creative work. Business lawyers help companies register copyrights and enforce them. This process is critical to making sure that a business retains control of its work in order to commercialize it for a profit.

Taxes

Businesses pay taxes. There are estimated taxes, employee taxes and deductions to be aware of. In addition to helping a business comply with tax requirements, a business lawyer helps their client take legal steps to minimize their tax burden. They may help the business apply for special tax forgiveness or waivers that might be available in a certain location or for certain industries.

Bankruptcy

Lawyers help businesses in both good times and bad. When businesses go through financial difficulties, they need lawyers to help them determine their options. Filing bankruptcy might be the only option or the best option for a struggling business.Making the decision to file for bankruptcy is just the beginning. There are many different types of bankruptcy filings available to businesses. They have different requirements, and there might be a reason that a business should choose one type of filing over another. Business lawyers can give their clients advice on the pros and cons of different actions. Once the business makes a plan, lawyers can help the company complete the filing accurately and stay in compliance with the associated requirements.

Why does need competition law ?

Competition law is a law that promotes or seeks to maintain market competition by regulating anti-competitive conduct by companies.Competition law is implemented through public and private enforcement. Competition law is known as antitrust law in the United States for historical reasons, and as "anti-monopoly law" in China and Russia. In previous years it has been known as trade practices law in the United Kingdom and Australia. In the European Union, it is referred to as both antitrust and competition law.

The history of competition law reaches back to the Roman Empire. The business practices of market traders, guilds and governments have always been subject to scrutiny, and sometimes severe sanctions. Since the 20th century, competition law has become global.The two largest and most influential systems of competition regulation are United States antitrust law and European Union competition law. National and regional competition authorities across the world have formed international support and enforcement networks.

Modern competition law has historically evolved on a country level to promote and maintain fair competition in markets principally within the territorial boundaries of nation-states. National competition law usually does not cover activity beyond territorial borders unless it has significant effects at nation-state level.Countries may allow for extraterritorial jurisdiction in competition cases based on so-called effects doctrine.The protection of international competition is governed by international competition agreements. In 1945, during the negotiations preceding the adoption of the General Agreement on Tariffs and Trade (GATT) in 1947, limited international competition obligations were proposed within the Charter for an International Trade Organisation. These obligations were not included in GATT, but in 1994, with the conclusion of the Uruguay Round of GATT Multilateral Negotiations, the World Trade Organization (WTO) was created. The Agreement Establishing the WTO included a range of limited provisions on various cross-border competition issues on a sector specific basis.

Competition law is a law that promotes or seeks to maintain market competition by regulating anti-competitive conduct by companies. Competition law is implemented through public and private enforcement. Competition law is known as antitrust law in the United States for historical reasons, and as "anti-monopoly law" in China and Russia. In previous years it has been known as trade practices law in the United Kingdom and Australia. In the European Union, it is referred to as both antitrust and competition law.

International expansion

By 2008, 111 countries had enacted competition laws, which is more than 50 percent of countries with a population exceeding 80,000 people. 81 of the 111 countries had adopted their competition laws in the past 20 years, signaling the spread of competition law following the collapse of the Soviet Union and the expansion of the European Union.Currently competition authorities of many states closely co-operate, on everyday basis, with foreign counterparts in their enforcement efforts, also in such key area as information / evidence sharing

Competition law rule

Competition law is affected by both British and European elements. The Competition Act 1998 and the Enterprise Act 2002 are the most important statutes for cases with a purely national dimension. However, if the effect of a business‘ conduct would reach across borders, the European Commission has competence to deal with the problems, and exclusively EU law would apply. Even so, the section 60 of the Competition Act 1998 provides that UK rules are to be applied in line with European jurisprudence. Like all competition law, that in the UK has three main tasks.

Prohibiting agreements or practices that restrict free trading and competition between business entities. This includes in particular the repression of cartels.
banning abusive behaviour by a firm dominating a market, or anti-competitive practices that tend to lead to such a dominant position. Practices controlled in this way may include predatory pricing, tying, price gouging, refusal to deal and many others. The mergers and acquisitions of large corporations, including some joint ventures. Transactions that are considered to threaten the competitive process can be prohibited altogether, or approved subject to "remedies" such as an obligation to divest part of the merged business or to offer licences or access to facilities to enable other businesses to continue competing.

The Competition and Markets Authority enforces competition law on behalf of the public. It merged the Office of Fair Trading with the Competition Commission after the Enterprise and Regulatory Reform Act 2013 Part 3. Consumer welfare and the public interest are the main objective of competition law, including industrial policy, regional development, protection of the environment and the running of public services. Competition law is closely connected with law on deregulation of access to markets, state aids and subsidies, the privatisation of state owned assets and the establishment of independent sector regulators. Specific "watchdog" agencies such as Ofgem, Ofcom and Ofwat are charged with seeing how the operation of those specific markets work.

Competition law, or antitrust law, has three main elements:

Prohibiting agreements or practices that restrict free trading and competition between business. This includes in particular the repression of free trade caused by cartels,banning abusive behavior by a firm dominating a market, or anti-competitive practices that tend to lead to such a dominant position. Practices controlled in this way may include predatory pricing, tying, price gouging, refusal to deal, and many others.

Supervising the mergers and acquisitions of large corporations, including some joint ventures. Transactions that are considered to threaten the competitive process can be prohibited altogether, or approved subject to "remedies" such as an obligation to divest part of the merged business or to offer licenses or access to facilities to enable other businesses to continue competing.

Substance and practice of competition law varies from jurisdiction to jurisdiction. Protecting the interests of consumers (consumer welfare) and ensuring that entrepreneurs have an opportunity to compete in the market economy are often treated as important objectives.

Competition law is closely connected with law on deregulation of access to markets, state aids and subsidies, the privatization of state owned assets and the establishment of independent sector regulators, among other market-oriented supply-side policies. In recent decades, competition law has been viewed as a way to provide better public services.

Competing Fairly: Why Businesses Need to Know about Competition Law ?

Firms involved in anti-competitive behaviour may find their agreements to be unenforceable and risk being fined up to 10% of group global turnover for particularly damaging conduct as well as exposing themselves to possible damages actions. Furthermore, individuals could also find themselves facing director disqualification orders or even criminal sanctions for serious breaches of competition law (see Out-Law's guide to Individual liability for competition law infringements). As such, any business - whatever its legal status, size and sector - needs to be aware of competition law, firstly so that it can meet its obligations (and in doing so, avoid the penalties mentioned above), but also so it can assert its own rights and protect its position in the marketplace.

In the UK two sets of competition rules currently apply in parallel. Anti-competitive behaviour which may affect trade within the UK is specifically prohibited by Chapters I and II of the Competition Act 1998 and the Enterprise Act 2002. Where the effect of anti-competitive behaviour extends beyond the UK to other EU Member States, it is prohibited by Articles 101 and 102 of the Treaty on the Functioning of the European Union (TFEU).

UK and EU competition law prohibit two main types of anti-competitive activity:

•anti-competitive agreements (under the Chapter I /

Article 101 prohibitions);
•and abuse of a dominant market position (under the Chapter II / Article 102 prohibitions).

The UK government has said it will make no fundamental changes to its competition law regime after the UK leaves the EU. Even after Brexit, or after any transition period, UK companies whose activities may affect trade within the EU, will remain subject to EU competition law.

Anti-competitive agreements (Chapter I / Article 101)

Both UK and EU competition law prohibit agreements, arrangements and concerted business practices which appreciably prevent, restrict or distort competition (or where this is the intended result) and which affect or may affect trade within the UK or the EU respectively.

Consequences of breach

Contravention of Chapter I or Article 101 can have serious consequences for a company:
•firms engaged in activities which breach these provisions can face fines of up to 10% of group global turnover;
•provisions in agreements which breach Chapter I or Article 101 are void and unenforceable (which may lead to the entire agreement being unenforceable);
•firms in breach of Chapter I or Article 101 also leave themselves exposed to actions for damages from customers and competitors who can show they have been harmed by the anti-competitive behaviour; and
•breach of Chapter I can result in individuals being disqualified from being a company director and lead to criminal sanctions.

Types of agreement caught

Whether an arrangement is anti-competitive is assessed on the basis of its objective, or its effect on competition, rather than its wording or form. This means that verbal and informal 'gentlemen's agreements' are equally capable of being found to be anti-competitive as formal, written agreements. Examples of the types of arrangement which are generally prohibited under Chapter I and Article 101 include:

•agreements which directly or indirectly fix purchase or selling prices, or any other trading conditions (for example, discounts or rebates, etc);

•agreements which limit or control production, markets, technical development or investment (for example, setting quotas or levels of output);

•agreements which share markets or sources of supply; and

•agreements which apply dissimilar conditions to similar transactions, placing other trading parties at a disadvantage.

Cartels

Cartel behaviour between competitors is the most serious form of anti-competitive behaviour under Chapter I or Article 101 and carries the highest penalties. A 'hardcore' cartel is one which involves price-fixing, market sharing, bid rigging or limiting the supply or production of goods or services. Individuals prosecuted for a cartel may be liable to imprisonment for up to five years and/or the imposition of unlimited fines.

Exemptions

The fact that an agreement is restrictive of competition does not mean that it is automatically prohibited (unless it is a hardcore cartel, see above). It may be that an agreement which appears to fall within the prohibitions under Chapter I or Article 101 is excluded or exempted from the competition rules.For example, an agreement which would otherwise be caught by Article 101 may be assumed to be harmless where the parties to it have market shares sufficiently low that there can be no real effect on competition or trade between Member States. The same principle is considered to apply, by analogy, to agreements otherwise caught by Chapter I. However, agreements which are deemed restrictive by object will almost always be found to infringe the competition rules. Other agreements may, nonetheless, be exempted under a 'block exemption' – a group exemption, which automatically exempts agreements falling within its terms. Different block exemptions may apply depending on the nature of the agreement or the market sector concerned.

Each sets out certain criteria (for example, relating to the market share of the parties and the types of restriction contained within the agreement) which must be met in order for an agreement to be block exempted. Even if an agreement does not fit squarely within a block exemption, it is still not automatically unlawful or unenforceable. An agreement may be individually exempted on the grounds that the restrictions of competition are outweighed by its beneficial effects.

For example, an agreement between two pharmaceutical companies to develop a new drug together as opposed to independently is likely to be subject to the Chapter I or Article 101 prohibition, as the two companies working together can be seen to reduce the number of products likely to be produced, by preventing each company from working on independent projects. However, the benefits for consumers resulting from such co-operation (i.e. more investment, leading to better drugs which reach the market faster), may be considered sufficient to off-set any anti-competitive effects.

Abuse of a dominant market position (Chapter II / Article 102 prohibition)

Both UK and EU competition law prohibit businesses with significant market power unfairly exploiting their strong market positions.

Consequences of breach

Contravention of Chapter II or Article 102 can have serious consequences for a company:

•firms engaged in activities which breach these provisions can face fines of up to 10% of group global turnover;

•conduct in breach of Chapter II or Article 102 can be stopped by court injunction;

•firms in breach of Chapter II or Article 102 also leave themselves exposed to actions from third parties who can show they have suffered loss as a result of the anti-competitive behaviour; and

•breach of Chapter II can result in individuals being disqualified from being a company director.

Type of behaviour caught

To be in a position of dominance, a business must have the ability to act independently of its customers, competitors and consumers. Establishing if a company is dominant requires a complex assessment of a number of elements but, as a general rule, if a business has a 50% market share there is a presumption that it is dominant. However, dominance has been found to exist where market share is as low as 40%.

Article 102 requires dominance in a substantial part of the European Union, but there is no requirement under Chapter II that a dominant position must be held in a substantial part of the UK, meaning that, in theory at least, dominance could be considered to exist in a fairly small area of the UK.

However, having a dominant position does not in itself breach competition law. It is the abuse of that position that is prohibited. Examples of behaviour that could amount to an abuse by a business of its dominant position include:

•imposing unfair trading terms, such as exclusivity;
•excessive, predatory or discriminatory pricing;
•refusal to supply or provide access to essential facilities; and
•tying (i.e. stipulating that a buyer wishing to purchase one product must also purchase all or some of his requirements for a second product from the dominant supplier).

Exemptions

There is no equivalent to the exemption for anti-competitive agreements, whereby a firm's conduct may be exonerated because of some compensating benefit. However, a dominant company may be able to show that it has an objective justification for otherwise abusive behaviour in certain circumstances. For example, a company may refuse to supply to a particular customer based on its poor credit rating, which would amount to the protection of legitimate business interests and not, therefore, to abusive conduct under Chapter II or Article 102. It would only be when such behaviour goes beyond what is necessary to protect the business' interests that this would amount to abuse.

Enforcement of competition law

For as long as the UK remains a member of the EU, UK competition authorities and courts are empowered to apply and enforce the entirety of Articles 101 and 102 of the TFEU, in addition to their existing powers to enforce the Competition Act 1998. The CMA is the principal competition law enforcement authority in the UK, though there are a number of sectoral regulatory authorities with concurrent powers to enforce competition laws in their respective sectors (for example, OFGEM for the electricity sector and OFWAT for the water sector). The risks associated with being a party to an anti-competitive agreement or abusing a dominant position are serious. In addition to the consequences already highlighted in this article (substantial fines, void and unenforceable agreements, damages actions and criminal sanctions for individuals in certain circumstances), a further key deterrent for businesses is the major disruption and damage to a company's reputation which arise from lengthy investigations or subsequent litigation from customers, competitors and consumers.

Achieving compliance

In view of the severe consequences of non-compliance, we recommend that businesses regularly review whether the company's practices and agreements comply with competition law. For any company (and especially any company with a significant share of the markets in which it is active), it is vitally important to promote an understanding amongst employees as to what type of behaviour is and is not permissible under competition law.

● Hong Kong competition law source

Why does Kong Kong needs Competition law? Competition law influences to many Asia countries accept this competitive legal to apply to protect businessmen have fair competition in themselves business market. Such as Hong Kong competition law starts in short time.

On 19 October 2018, the Hong Kong Competition Commission (HKCC) decided that the Code of Banking Practice (Code) has to comply with the First Conduct Rule, which prohibits undertakings and associations of undertakings from agreeing or making decisions which have the object or effect of restricting competition in Hong Kong.

The Hong Kong Monetary Authority (HKMA) approved Code is an industry code of practice issued by the DTC Association and the Hong Kong Association of Banks. Amongst others, the Code requires banks, in certain circumstances, not to impose various fees and charges, charge customers multiple credit card fees or allow customers' credit card debts to exceed certain amounts.

In December 2017, 14 institutions authorised under the Banking Ordinance submitted an application (Application) arguing that the Code should be excluded from the First Conduct Rule by reason of section 2 of Schedule 1 of the Competition Ordinance, which excludes the First Conduct Rule from applying to "any agreement to the extent that it is made for the purpose of complying with a legal requirement...imposed by or under any enactment in force in Hong Kong".

The HKCC took the view that the legal requirement exclusion did not apply as the Code was not a legal requirement imposed by or under the Banking Ordinance. Importantly, the HKCC expressly stated that it has not decided if the Code infringes the First Conduct Rule, as this was not part of the Application. Nonetheless, as a matter of enforcement policy, the HKCC currently does not intend to investigate or enforce against the Code as it "may in fact benefit customers...is intended to promote good banking practices towards customers, and has been formulated with the input and support of the Consumer Council and the HKMA".

Hong Kong regulator needs more enforcement experience before making big changes to competition rules, commissioner says by Freny Patel, PaRR

•Local adaptation difficult as competition law principles apply generally

•Interlocking directorate less examined issue in competition law

•No major wholesale changes to guidelines anticipated given paucity of time

Hong Kong's Competition Commission will need much more enforcement experience than it currently possesses to make major adaptations to the city's draft competition guidelines, released on 9 October, says Thomas Cheng, a member of the commission.

Hong Kong president comments come in the wake of criticism by some antitrust lawyers that the guidelines mirror those prevailing in Europe and do not necessarily reflect local circumstances.

A Hong Kong-based antitrust lawyer said that although the commission had taken a lot from Europe when drafting the guidelines, the guidelines needed to more faithfully reflect the characteristics of the Hong Kong market. The lawyer said Hong Kong was largely a distribution centre and a relatively small economy with many family-owned businesses and interlocking directorates.

Hong Kong president told PaRR that local adaptation was always a difficult issue, considering that competition law principles were meant to apply generally.

The Hong Kong president said major adaptations were generally necessary only if there were fundamental differences between the local economy and other advanced competition law jurisdictions from which legal principles are derived, such as different levels of economic development or if there were substantial state ownership in the economy, as in the case of China.

Detecting abuse of dominance

Determing when a firm's behaviour is an abuse of market power, as opposed to a competitive action, is one of the most complex and controversial areas in competition policy. Competition laws typically contain provisions prohibiting abuse of market power by dominant firms or attempts of not yet dominant firms to monopolise markets. However, there is considerable divergence among jurisdictions about the precise definition of dominance, the range of practices and conducts that should be condemned as anti-competitive, and finally the choice of remedies that should be imposed. Examples of abusive practices typically include:

•predatory pricing
•loyalty rebates
•tying and bundling
•refusals to deal
•margin squeeze
•excessive pricing

A proper understanding of when a firm's actions could be considered abusive is important for competition authorities because consumers'and the economy would be harmed by an incorrect intervention. A firm with a large market share, which might be considered dominant, also needs to understand the law and economics in this area, which is not always easy.

Mergers: An integral part of the competition landscape to be closely monitored. Almost all systems of competition law provide for control of mergers, to prevent companies from joining together to eliminate competition between them.

A merger could be a complete union of two or more companies, a more one-sided takeover or the transfer of parts of one firm to another. Deciding whether a merger will harm competition can require sophisticated economic analysis of markets and the effects of the transaction. Yet this sophisticated analysis must in most jurisdictions be carried out to strict deadlines so as to protect the procedural rights of all affected parties.

Why do competition authorities analyse mergers?

Most mergers are beneficial to competition, or at least do no harm to it, so competition authorities typically conduct a quick screening exercise to identify the exceptions. In, mergers between competitors can result in very large costs to consumers and to the economy more generally, so it is essential that authorities have the power and skills to investigate effectively and to remedy any potential problems they find (including by blocking the merger).

Mergers between companies that do not directly compete (such as a 'vertical' merger between a supplier and its customer) rarely raise competition concerns; but when they do, they require very sophisticated economic analysis to assess whether the effects are anti-competitive or efficiency-enhancing.

What are cartels and how do they affect consumers?

Hard core cartels (when firms agree not to compete with one another) are the most serious violations of competition law. They injure customers by raising prices and restricting supply, thus making goods and services completely unavailable to some purchasers and unnecessarily expensive for others.

The categories of conduct most often defined as hard core cartels are:

•price fixing

•output restrictions

•market allocation

•bid rigging (the submission of collusive tenders)

Hard core cartel prosecution is a priority policy objective for the OECD. Increasingly, prohibition against hard core cartels is now considered to be an indispensable part of a domestic competition law.

Challenges in detecting hard core cartels

Cartels are very difficult to detect. They can involve many firms in the industry and customers are rarely in a position to detect the existence of a cartel. Antitrust enforcers should be helped in their ability to detect cartels by various means and instruments, the most effective being leniency programmes. These programmes provide immunity or reduction in sanctions for cartel members that co-operate (or 'whistleblow') with competition enforcers. Leniency programmes have been adopted by most OECD countries and have been instrumental in increasing the success rate of the detection of cartels.

The best outcomes are secured by deterring firms from forming cartels in the first place. Strong sanctions are therefore a fundamental component of an effective antitrust enforcement policy against hard core cartels. An important supplement to fines against organisations for cartel conduct is sanctions against individuals for their participation in the conspiracy. These sanctions can take the form of substantial administrative fines or, in some countries, the criminal sanction of imprisonment. The prospect of incarceration can be a powerful deterrent for businesspeople considering entering into a cartel agreement.

But are all agreements among competitors harmful?

Some horizontal agreements between companies can fall short of a hard core cartel, and in certain cases may have beneficial effects. For example, agreements between competitors related to research & development, production and marketing can result in reduced costs for companies, or improved products, the benefits of which are passed on to consumers. The challenge for competition authorities is how to assess these agreements, balancing the pro-competitive effects against any anti-competitive effects which may distort the market.

Governments should consider competition, and its potential benefits, across the whole range of their policies. Establishing a framework of competition law and liberalising sectors is important, but so is assessing the competitive effects of regulations and government intervention in other policy areas.

Why do governments need competition law?

All types of government policies can affect market competition, for good or bad. Governments should ensure that social or other policies that are not intended to damage market competition do not do so unnecessarily or by accident. For example, if policies to enforce product standards or to ensure provision of essential goods, are badly designed, they might cause higher prices or worsen the quality of services for consumers.

In some instances, policies restricting competition are the result of businesses lobbying to avoid competition, in other cases they may simply be the result of insufficient assessment being carried out at the policy design stage. In many cases, alternative approaches can be found to achieve the policy's purpose, while avoiding unnecessary restrictions of competition.

Competition can also be used to make policy more effective. Many governments have discovered that they can use markets for more efficient policy delivery – for example, by establishing markets in pollution rights, to meet environmental targets at least cost.

Effective competition policy requires effective and efficient application of competition law and economics. Much of the work carried out by the OECD focuses on the background and framework of competition policy, and how competition authorities can learn from each other and from academic work to improve their effectiveness.

Processes and economic analysis: key to effective competition policy

Good processes are essential: a fair, predictable and transparent process bolsters the legitimacy of a competition authority's actions. Whatever the legal framework, consistency, predictability and fairness in decision-making processes can be fostered by transparency about legal standards, agency policies, practices and procedures as well as the judicial review process.

Good economic analysis is also necessary. Any assessment of competition, whether carried out for law enforcement or wider policy purposes, will require a sound understanding of economic principles, and based on careful analysis of the evidence, possibly including statistical and other techniques for the analysis of data. This analysis need not be sophisticated, but all competition professionals need to be prepared to consider and use sophisticated econometric or other techniques where needed, or to respond to evidence of this sort presented by interested parties.

On conclusion, a competitive market environment that allows new firms to challenge incumbents, efficient firms to grow and inefficient ones to exit can help boost economic growth and living standards.

CHAPTER V

Law case research

(1) Sale of property case (contract law)

This case concerns whether the property seller had mislead the property buyer to sign contract to buy the property in UK. This is judgement in (i) a claim principally relating to a UK property sale and (ii) a counterclaim by the UK property seller for what are outstanding sums under a bridging loan agreement between the UK property buyer and UK property left a both parties, because the sale of the UK property left a shortfall on the sums due to the UK property buyer. This case follows UK contract law to judge whether UK property buyer can compensate a claim developer (seller) can receive a counterclaim for what are outstanding sums under a bridging loan agreement from the UK property buyer.

The final judgement concludes that in fact, the UK property seller mislead to persuade the UK property purchase to make the final decision to sign the contract to purchase the UK property. Hence, the UK property seller breaches the contract law agreement and the UK property purchaser can sue the UK property developer (seller) successfully to refund all the full payment for the property purchase and the UK property purchaser does not pay a counterclaim of the outstanding sums under a bridging loan agreement to the UK property developer (seller). I shall indicate the factual background and judgement reasons as below:

Fact background

The UK property developer indicated the property for the

price stated UK$600,000.00 and the property purchase price was raised in part by a loan of UK$60,000.00 from one bank which loan was secured by first legal charge over the property. The bank has these requirements to the property purchaser if he hopes to be accepted to borrow the property loan. The requirements include as below:

(1) The UK property purchaser will need to agree in a separate document (the certificates of the intended letting) to let out the dwellings for five years following the final payment to pay to property seller.

(2) The UK property buyer must retain the ownership of the property for five years at least following the final payment of the property.

(3) The bank loan for property purchaser must have been approved to the UK property buyer and the UK property developer(seller) before the bank and the property buyer sign the loan contract. If any of the conditions set out above are breached , then the bank can recover all loan lending and interest charged amount from the UK property buyer.

On 20 th April 2019, a sale memorandum for the property was issued by the property seller (developer), its one estate agent. The prospective property purchaser was identified to let it to know the property sale price was said to be UK$600,000.00 The following were further forms of the sale as recorded in the memorandum. A deposit of UK$100,000.00 from the UK property sale price of UK$600,000.00 of the said deposit will be released to the property seller in order to let him to pay the contractor to complete the building work being completed and signed off. At the same time, because the bank loan was due to expire, the property buyer was trying to obtain a bridging loan to repay bank and to complete the property development. Because the property buyer's conditions are accepted to the property developer. So, the bank accepted his bank loan application to buy the UK developer's one property as well as the UK property developer also issues one property purchase and sale contract and offer letter and one bank loan application acceptance offer letter and bank loan contract both are made clear though that the UK property purchase offer and UK bank loan offer both were subject to the property buyer's due diligence amongst other matters.

They mean that the UK property buyer ensures to accept the UK property seller and the UK bank to whose property purchase offer and bank loan offer after he decided to sign their contracts.

Why do this UK property seller and thus UK property bank both mislead this UK property to sign their contracts? The reasons may include that they had ever done those behaviors to mislead this UK property buyer to sign their contracts as below:

(1) The purchase property development appeared not to have PROGRESSED some months.

(2) The development of the flats was basically completed , but they would need to be redecorated.

(3) The development displayed two serious defects, namely, the incorrect installation of the stairs which work ultimately require the first floor levels to be adjusted , but that this defect would be remedied free of charge by the contractors and the flat roof had been formed incorrectly resulting in water penetration.

(4) The property seller estimated the cost of finishing the work was UK$15,000.00 and he told to the property buyer before, but after the property buyer signs the property purchase and sale contract. The property seller would state that finishing the work would run to at least UK$50,000.00 ,

but potentially UK$75,000.00 taking into consideration the above.
(5) Then, the property seller valued that property at UK one million taking into account the remedial works.
Thus, the property price raised to UK one million from UK$600,000.00. It increased UK$400,000.00 ,due to the development period displayed these two serious defects. However, the UK property seller told the UK property buyer, he can not predict when these two serious defects occurrence and why their defects occurrence in this property development period. Hence, the UK property buyer needs to pay UK one million to this UK property. However, the UK property buyer's purchase contract and bank loan contract are not valued (effective) , because the UK property seller's negligence to cause serious defects to bring the property price is increased. It is not the property buyer's responsibility to compensate his defect loss. So, the property buyer does not breach the property purchase and bank loan both contracts.
Consequently, the UK property seller can not sue the UK property buyer to compensate his extra defects loss cost successfully, because these both UK property purchase and bank loan contracts are nor effective and the UK property buyer had not breached these both contracts as well as it seems that the UK property seller and bank had mislead the purchase buyer to sign their contracts.

(2) Breach of contract artist case
An artist has a contract with an art gallery, to exhibit whose paintings for an agreed period of time. The art gallery cancels the act exhibition before that period of time expires. The artist sues the art gallery for breach of contract. The art gallery counterclaims against the artist,

also for breach of contract, for failing to provide to the art gallery himself for the purpose of the exhibition, the agreed quantity and quality of paintings as well as the art gallery also wants to claim against , another art gallery for inducing the artist's breach of contract with the art gallery himself.
The first art gallery says that the artist has exhibited paintings in the second's gallery contrary to a clause in the contract between the artist and the first art gallery themselves, restricting the extent to which the artists could exhibit paintings in any other gallery during the life of contract between the artist and the fist art gallery.
As the first art gallery has counterclaim against the artist in the main action, and wants to claim against a person not already a party in respect of the same subject-matter of the counterclaim (the artist's beach of its contract with the first art gallery). The first art gallery can add the second art gallery as a defendant to the counterclaim.
It indicated that this procedure should be contrasted with the procedure to add third parties in existing action. A defendant who wants to claim against someone other than the plaintiff and who does not also want to counterclaim against the plaintiff in the main action.

(3) Breach of contract artist case

The plaintiff artist gave some of her paintings to an art gallery in France. The gallery later returned them to her in gallery in Hong Kong by shipping them with Nippon France. Upon arrival Hong Kong by shipping them with received by Nippon HK (Nippon HK) as agent for Nippon France. The plaintiff refused to pay Nippon HK, due to the plaintiff artist feels the Paris art gallery had shipped the paintings in breach of its contract with the plaintiff. The plaintiff sued Nippon HK , because the paintings were wrongfully held and demanding their return. Nippon HK applied for the addition or substitution of Nippon France as a defendant. The HK court of appeal said the resolution of the dispute as to which of the two Nippon (HK) and France companies were the carrier of the paintings, and this should be determined in the same action.

In this example, adding Nippon (France) was preferable to substituting it for Nippon (HK) because at trial , one or the other of the companies could have been found to be the carrier of the paintings. Their presence before the court at the same time and in the same action was therefore the most just and convenient way to resolve all of the issues related to the wrongful detention of the paintings.

(4) A share in the estate of the plaintiff's deceased father case (family law) case

The plaintiff and defendant were involved in third party proceedings, in which the issue was whether the defendant was a brother of the plaintiff and therefore entitled to share in the estate of the plaintiff's deceased father. The plaintiff then commenced an action for discovery against an university to obtain certain documents which he said were relevant to the issue of the true parentage of the defendant. The plaintiff wanted the documents prior to the trial. So that he could have their analysis by a handwriting expert to prove. But the defendant applied family law rule to intervene and to be joined as a defendant in the university (handwriting expert) discovery action.

The court refused his application because he could have an opportunity during the trial of the third party proceedings to be heard on any matter relating to the admissibility of the documents. The issue as between plaintiff and the university was simply whether the plaintiff was entitled to discovery of the documents, prior to the trial , and the defendant had no legitimate interest to protect that made intervention necessary . Giving leave to the defendant to intervene would tend to increase rather than prevent a multiplicity of contested proceedings.

(5) Family law concerns shares owning authority in the name of plaintiff's deceased sister case

IN an action regarding the status of certain shares. Plaintiff applied to be substituted in place of the two existing plaintiffs in the action. He contended that shares in the name of his deceased sister has been held by his brother in trust for their deceased mother and should therefore form part of the mother's estate. His interest in the matter was that he was a beneficiary under his mother's will. He wanted to replace the two existing plaintiffs, who were the executors of the mother's estate.

Those plaintiff executors were unwilling to pursue the claim that the shares should be part of the mother's estate because they were afraid the estate would have to beat the costs of any unsuccessful litigation . They were , however, willing to be replaced as plaintiffs by the decreased mother's son plaintiff and to be joined as defendants. The decreased mother's son plaintiff was substituted as plaintiff for the two executors, who were estate property administered and applied for his benefit, and the executors had refused to continue with the action.

(6) Employment law, employee claims compensation for illness case.

The plaintiff was a printing worker employed by the defendant printing company. Chemical solvent was used in the defendant's printing business. The plaintiff developed a neurological illness as a result of prolonged exposure to a particular chemical in the solvent. IN addition of the printing worker sued his printing company for compensation for illness during he had gotten illness from chemical solvent material, due to he needed to contact this material when he was working. He also sued Shell company, supplied the chemical solvent to his employer to cause his illness to compensate his body illness.

The Shell company conducted its defense if it were added as a defendant. As Shell company had already been made a third party and was activity preparing its case, there was no question of Shell company facing a claim. The court ordered Shell company to be added as a defendant.

Contract can negligent demolition work claim case and tort as a result of damage to its property caused by negligent demolition work. One of the defendants was the owner of the building and was sued by the plaintiff under a strict liability. That defendant served contribution notices on the contractor and sub-contractor (co0defendants) who carried out or were responsible for the demolition that caused the damage to the plaintiff's property.

(7) Family law, sex discrimination equal treatment case. Various parties brought actions in which they alleged discrimination on the basis of sex. The equal opportunities commission asked for leave to appear at the appeal stage because the appeals involved issues rating to provisions of the sex discrimination ordinance and probably because it doubted whether the defendants would be represented . The requested have was granted.

(8) Family law, who is divorce proceedings advisor case.

One husband in divorce proceedings, used his sister as an advisor. The role of his sister because more active in the proceeding, especially after the husband became too ill to represent himself. His wife and applicant had not at first objected to his sister's role as an advisor, but began to express concerns to the court as his sister's role became more active. The court also had concerns about the role of his sister having developed to the point that his sister was very much the barrister in the case. There was animosity between his sister and the divorced husband's wife, which meant that his sister could never be an independent third party with professionally detached objectivity. The court left his sister in place as his brother (divorced husband) 's advisor subject to a reconsideration of the issue as the matter progressed.

(9) Business law, suing bank compensation case.

A seller and a buyer are respectively under a purchase order. Both had bank accounts with a bank and both had agreed with the bank that the product would be paid for a transfer from the seller's bank account to the buyer's bank account.

A dispute then arose between the seller and the buyer , as a result of which the seller cancelled the purchase order. The seller failed to inform the bank, and the bank debited the seller's account as previously agreed. The seller asked the bank and the bank agreed .The seller asked the bank and the seller refused.

The buyer demanded return of the funds. Bank tried to get the seller's approval to do, but the seller refused. The buyer then threatened to sue the bank and then the bank froze the seller's bank account.

The buyer sued the bank for wrongfully transferring duns from the buyer's to the seller's bank account. The seller sued the bank for freezing its bank account also.

The bank applied for interpleads relief. The application was dismissed by a master and a judge. The bank had got itself in trouble with the buyer by the re-debit his bank account action and has got itself in trouble with the seller by freezing the seller's bank account. It could not extricate itself from those problems and the resulting lawsuits by applying for interpleader relief. The requirement of lack of collusion had not been met.

(10) Breach sale of property contract claim to the firm of solicitors case.

One defendant firm of solicitors failed to register a sale and purchase agreement between the plaintiff purchaser and developer relating to a flat in a planned land development. The building was never completed and the developer on-sold the land before. A term of the sale was that outstanding rules agreements were to be cancelled (and deposits returned) to ensure the purchaser took the land free.

After the plaintiff sued his solicitors for their failure in the past to register the sale and purchase agreement, pleading breach of contract and negligence, it was held that the claim in contract was time-barred.

When solicitors did something contrary to the terms of their retainer, the time for bringing proceedings for breach of contract began to run from the date of that ask, likewise, then solicitors omitted to do something required, the breach occurred when they failed to do the act that they had been engaged to do.

The fact that they could have remedied that breach meant only that they could have proved the consequences of that breach and did not mean that the duty to register continued until the date when effective registration became impossible . However, neither ignorance of the law nor the inability to pay legal costs , due to financial difficulty constitutes a valid ground for extending the relevant limitation period in contract.

The judgement bases on this reason: The general rule in negligence actions is that the plaintiff has to prove that the defendant is liable for wrongful conduct as a result of which the plaintiff has been damaged. Time runs from the date on which the damage is proved. This has presented problems, particularly , in the case of building work, e.g. where the conduct complained of is negligence in the contraction of a house, the plaintiff may only become aware of it, when cracks first start to appear in the walls some years. Later, what is the date from which the cause of action arises and the limitation period starts to accrue?

There are a number of possibilities, such as the date on which the construction was completed, the date on which the cracks first started to appear, and the date on which the cracks first came to the plaintiff's actual attention. Where the plaintiff sues his solicitor for negligent advice. The date on which the plaintiff suffered the damage is the relevant date for the commencement of the limitation period. What is the position where the plaintiff is unaware that he has a cause of action until the six year time bar has expired?

(11) Employment contract and tort concerns worker's injury claim case.

Knowledge of the injury to employees of the following facts need to include:

That that injury in question whether was significant and that the injury was attributable in whole or in part to the act is caused by negligence, nuisance or breach of duty and the identify of the defendant and if it is caused that the act was that of a person (worker) and the additional facts supporting the bringing of an action against the defendant. Whether the plaintiff knew that the act involved negligence, nuisance as breach of duty in the legal sense is not relevant and can not postpone time from running.

Whether an injury is " significant" is viewed objectively, and the plaintiff is expected to know facts that he could observe or ascertain himself or with the help of expert advice, if it would have been reasonable to obtain it.

Before last year, the plaintiff injured his back during the cause of his employment as a student nurse at one hospital. He was treated for a sprained back and returned to work after 13 days' sick leave. IN this year, he received employees' compensation. However, he continued to suffer from back pain and he had an operation at this moment, pursued a further employees' compensation claim, but little was done about it. Later , he was granted legal aid and a writ was issued. He applied to the court for the three years limitation period to be applied, giving the following reasons for the delay to claim injury compensation.

He was preoccupied with seeking and receiving medical treatment, he was preoccupied with working as a nurse and he was preoccupied with seeking employees' compensation and did not know of his right to seek damage at common law.

His application was dismisses. Amongst the reasons given,. The court found as facts that neither the plaintiff's treatment , nor his work were such as to justify the length of delay. The prejudice to the plaintiff if his application was dismissed did not out weigh the prejudice that would be suffered by the defendant id the application that would be suffered by the defendant if the application was granted, particularly so given the difficulty of tracing witnesses and the likelihood of memories having faded so long after the incident.

(12) Applying the test, summary judgement application whether is dishonoured cheque claim case.

This case is not intended to be a mini-trial, the practice of using summary judgement application for this purpose has been strongly and repeatedly criticized and rejected by the court of appeal. A retailed consideration of relevant facts, document and legal issues is required.

One defendant issued a $200,000.00 cheque for the deposit on a purchase of a flat from the plaintiff. The cheque was later dishonoured. The plaintiff sued on the cheque and applied for summary judgement. One of the defenses was that " the purchase price of the flat had never been agreed " and that " the agreement has been signed with the part as to price left black." The judge found that this assertion was "simply unbelievable" . In reaching this view, he relied not only on the impossibility that the defendant would have signed insert the purchase price. He also relied on the defendant's copy of that agreement, which clearly demonstrated that the parties had inserted the purchase price.

In this example, the defense raised was contradicted by other documentary evidence and by the defendant's assertions. It is therefore appropriate to form a view of the defendant's credibility.

(13) Propery contract for occupy to earn profit unreal case

The plaintiff and defendant signed a provisional sales agreement and the plaintiff granted a licence to occupy the property until completion . Disputes acrose between the parties, as a result of which completion did not occur as scheduled . The plaintiff sued the defendant for possession of the property and for profits.

The defendant denied that if repudiated the agreement ans counterclaimed for spcific performance , alternatively for

damages . The plaintiff successfully applied for an intermin payment. The defendant appealed. The court of appeal allowed the
appeal because it wad not plain from the grounds advanced by the plaintiff that the plaintiff was bound to succeed
in recovering money at trial in respect of the defendant's use and occupation of the property.

(14) The defendant (landload) lets premises to the plaintiff (rentee) case.

The plaintiff sued the defendant on the basis that assurances given to the plaintiff by the defendant regarding the premises were untrue. The plaintiff wanted to continue to occupy the premises, but it sued for damages for breach of warranty. The defendant counterclaimed for possession, arrears of rent and profits in relation to the plaintiff's use and occupation of the premises and applied for an interim payment.

The court said that the defendant would be entitled to an interim payment only if she would succeed in defeating the plaintiff's claim at trial. The defendant was awarded an interim payment, part by lump sum for arrears of rent and part by way of periodical payments on account of rent or profits.

The defendants (rentees) were ordered to make an interim payment to the plaintiff (lanlord) in respect of the defendant's use and occupation of premises. The defendants appealed on the basis that the
amount of the interim payment ordered was too large. The defendants submitted on appeal that the interim payment should have been based on the reduced rent that the parties agreed , because of problems with the lifts in the building would be paid by the defendant, but on the rent as set out in the tenancy agreement.

The court of appeal found it was arguable that the rent payable by the defendant had been reduced by the plaintiff by agreement, and that the interim payment reduced rent, not on the rent as stated in
the tenancy agreement. The interim payment was reduced accordingly.

(15) Security for lawyer winner's cost case

The usual principle that the loser pays the winner's costs may be of little comfort to the defendant where it is unlikely that he will be able to recover his costs can only be made against a plaintiff or a person in the position of a plaintiff, such as a defendant who counterclaims, or a defendant who has issued a third party notice. If a defendant succeeds in his application for until the plaintiff complies with the order by paying the security in the manner ordered by the court.

When hearing an application for security costs, the court's primary concerns are whether the defendant has shown that he as sufficient grounds for making the application,
whether its discretion should be exercised by granting the order, and if the amount of security that the plaintiff should be ordered to provide.

For example, when a limited company is plaintiff in any action or other legal proceeding, any judge having jurisdiction in matter may, if it appears by credible
testimony that there is reason to believe that the company will be unable to pay the costs of the defendant if successful in his defense, require sufficient security to be given for thoser costs, and may stay all proceedings until the security is given.

Security cost against liquidator's expenses. The plaintiff companies were in liquidation, although some assets wewre available. Their action against the defandant firm of accountants was for breach of duty in connection with auditing of the plaintiff company's accounts. If the costs of the action were to rank with the other debts, the liquidators would not be able to meet the costs in any appreciable amount.

Security was granted and the plaintiffs appealed. The cost of appeal allowed the appeal because the evidence showed that the nature of the claim was such that the costs of the action should be treated as liquidator's expenses rather than debts, and the remaining assets would be sufficient to meet any likely order for costs. Furthermore, the liquidators undertook to inform the court of any change of suitation.

(16) Employment contract, medical negligence claim case

During the plaintiff's inordinate and inexcusable delay in prosecuting a medical negligence claim, the defendant's insurance arrangements changed. The result of the change was that the defendant, not its
insurers, would have to pay any damages awarded to the plaintiff. If there had been no delay, judgement would have been given sooner and the insurer would have
been responsible for satisfying the judgement. The causal link between the delay and the financial prejudice was proved, and the plaintiff's action was dismissed for want of prosecution.

(17) Wrongful dermination of an employment contract case.

The plaintiff sued the defendant for wrongful formation of an employment contract. The plaintiff was relying on an oral contract and it was accepted that the oral evidence of the
contract and it was accepted that the oral evidence of the parties and their witnesses would be vital if the case wants to trial. The oral evidence would relate to events that happened ten year earlier.

The judge found that there had been inordinate and inexcusable delay and that this would effect the possibility of a fair trial. He refused to dismiss the action, however, because the
defendant had seven years earlier, failed to comply with an order in the action to exchange witness statements (the plaintiff ahd also failed to comply with that order).

On appeal, the cost said it was proper for the judge to have taken into account the defendant's failure to prepare its own case and to comply with order to exchange
witness statements. However, even if the defendant had complied with the order, it would still have suffered prejudice because oral evidence was vital and would
relate to event that happened ten years agp. Furthermore, there had been signifcant amendments to the pleadings since the order to exchange witness statements had been made.

(18) Cost orders of discovery of documents to
whom solicot's fee case

Two days before, the trial , the plaintiff's solicitors asked the defendant's solicitors for correspondence relating to an agreement between the parties. The plaintiff was against the defendant that the agreement was a forgery. Upon receipt of the requested correspondence from the defendant, with established that the agreement was not a foregery, the plaintiff withdrew its action against the defendant. At not time prior to the plantiff's request two days before the trial had the plaintiff made any other respect for the documents or had the defendant disclosed them.

The solicitors no both sides had failed in their duty to ensure proper discovery was given the correspondence in question was not in the hands of the clients, who were entitled to assume that their respective solicitors would appreciate this issues in dispute, make proper and timely production and inquiries for documents, and receive the oppenent's list to assess whether there might be other relevant documents. Finally, cost orders were made against both solicitors.

(19) Sale of cigarettes contract discovery of documents requested case.

The plaintiff sued that it has a contract with the defendant for the sale of cigarettes. The plaintiff obtained an order requiring the defendant to disclose sales invoices and correspondence between the defendant and another company. The defendant said the requested documents belonged to a company , was associated with the defendant , but a separate legal entity.

The court of appeal refused to other the requested discovery for two reasons: cycle plaintiff had not raised as an issue in its pleadings that the company had any role in the breach of contract by the defendant and the fact that the request documents belonged to a " sistor or cousin company " od the defendant was not sufficient to establish that the defendant was not sufficient to establish that the defendant had the necessary control over the company to justify the discovery order.

In order for these plaintiffs to have obtained the requested discovery order, they would have shown , for example, that the day-to-day management of the related company was effectively in the hands of the defendant or that the two companies shared a common management and decision making structure that was dominated , or controlled by the defendant. No such evidence as presentd. When discovery is requested from an individual of documents in possession of a company , similar considerations apply. The court will look at the relationship between the individual and the company and ask if that individual has sufficient control over the affairs of the company to direct that the documents be disclosed.
The fact that a person is a shareholder of a company is that inclusive. However, if tht person is also a chairman and managing director of the company, this is persuasive evidence that he would have in his power all of the company's business documents in his capacity as chairman and managing director.

(20) Discovery of document is not necessary case to flight case
attendant union occupation of premise unlegal to
Cathay Pacific , breach of agreement case.

The plaintiff , Cathay Pacific sued the defendant flight attendants union to recovered possession of and profits -for-the occupation of premises which the plaintiff had allowed the union to occupy free of charge for many years. The defendant argued that the plaintiff's attempt to recover occupation was in breach of an agreement between parties. The defendant flight attenants union sought documents regarding Cathay Pacific's request to another Pacific Cathay uninion (the aircrew officer's union) to move that union's office. The defendant also sought all documents hold by

Cathay Pacific concerning review of Cathay Pacific's policy regarding all union accommodation.
The judge held that discovery of document is not
(1) the necessary reasons: documents regarding the aircrew officer's union were irrelevant to any issues between the parties and that even if they were relevant, they were not necessary for disposing fairly of the matter or for saving costs, and (2) that the plaintiff's policy regarding union commodation was irrelevant to the issues as pleaded. The court of appeal agreed , and added that the second request was excessively wide.

(21) Discovery of cocuments, accident report at work case. A employee died in an accident of work. His employer immediately arranged for an inquiry to be conducted into the circumstances of the accident. His wife , later sued the employer for damages as a result of her husband's death . She asked the employer for a copy of the accident inquiry report. The employer refused to disclose the report. The employer indicate that he did not need to prepare accident report for her husband's accident death reasons as below:
To establish the cause of the accident , so that appropriate safety measures could be taken ,and to obtain advice from the employer's solicitors to advice in the litigation that was almost certain to ensure, and that there two purposes were of equal weight. The employer was ordered to disclose report on the basis only if obtaining legal advice was the dominant purpose for preparing the report.
However, the employer is needed to deliver accident report , it bases on the reason, in determining the dominant purpose, one can consider not only the intention of document or other communication intention, but also the intention of the person who directed that the document

be created. In this case, legal advice is not dominant . The dominant purpose of communication is necessary. So, the employer needs to deliver a copy of the accident inquiry report to its employee's wife for his accident dath at work case.

(22) Civil law process case

An effectiveness of legal system is cost, timeliness, the quality of the judges and lawyers who work within it, the high court consists of the court of First instance , court of appeal. Case law (judicial precedent) is also an important source of procedure. In fact, it is impossible to understand procedural law without also being familiar with a large body of case law.

For Hong Kong civil law example, is litigation in HK the right method of solving the dispute? A review of the documents may reveal the presence of a binding foreign juisdiction clause or arbitration clause, effectively preventing procedings in HK.

For example, if the amount of the claim is small, an attempt to negotiate a settlement quickly, without resource to litigation, may be in the client's better interests. IS litigation appropriate, in which court should the proceedings be commenced? The high court has unlimited civil jurisdiction, although if a case is within the monetary jurisdiction of the distinct court. Is the debtor worth suing? The client may not have thought far beyond commencing proceedings, but there is little point in doing so if any judgement subsequently and expensively obtained can't be enforced because the defendant has no assets.

(23) The cost of litigation compensation case

The statement that civil litigation is a very expensing business is hardly news worthy. Although, solicitors know that it is impossible to anticipate with any degree of precision at the outset of an action the total cost of taking the case to trail, it is most unsatisfactory from the client's point of view. Therefore, as a matter of conduct, solicitors are obliged to explain as fully as possible the likely costs involved. Usually a successful party recovers approximately three -quarters of his costs upon taxation. For example, for security for costs, this will have the effect of staying the action until the security has be recorded in written form, both to assist the client's underatanding and to serve as a record for the solicitor's file.

However, certain proceedings are excluded , such as defemation actions (except defending a counterclaim defamation), partnership disputes , money claims of securities, currency futures and proceedings in labor Tribunal and small claims tribunal.

Civil proceedings in the high court may be begun by writ, originating summom, originating motion, or petition. The actions may include tort, fraud , breach of duty , contractual, leading to a claim for damages for personal injuries, patent infringement, a contentious probate action. Some proceedings must be begun by originating summons, e.g. proceedings by which an application is made to the High court or a High court Judge " under any written law" , e..g. some application under the trustee ordinance, the importance of good case management is an issue to avoid extra expense and delay in civil litigation. In adequate case management can have a detrimental effort not only on the parties to the litigation, but also on the court of inadequate case management include wasted time and unnecessary expenses.

Pleadings are the formal documents exchanged among parties to litigation in which the parties state all of the material facts that support their claims and defences.

Pleadings include the statement of claim, defence, counterclaim, reply, defence to counterclaim, further and better particulars and third party notice.

The formal requirements of pleading must include the year of issue of the writ, the number of the action description of the pleading and the date of service.

Drafting pleadings aims to inform the other side of the nature of the case , they have to meet as distinguished from the mde in which the case is to be proved, to prevent the other side from being taken by surprise at trial, to enable the other side to know what evidence they ought to be prepared with and to prepare for trial, to limit the generally of the pleading, generality of the pleading, the claim and the evidence interences or conclusions of law to be drawn from the material facts must not br stated in the pleadings.

The parties' task is to plead and prove facts, it is the judge, assisted by the parties' advocates,who will draw the legal conclusions. There are occasions whn it may be difficult to distinguish between a material fact and a conclusion of law. For example, in a claim for negligence , it is common to allege in a pleading the neglient conduct, this is very close to pleading a conclusion of law.

Every pleading must obtain the particulars of any claim , defence or other matter pleaded, including (bit not limited to) misrepresentation, fraud, breach of trust , mental incapacity, fraudulent intent, repudiation of contract, and acceptance repudiation.

In personal injury actions, the plaintiff id expected to serve with the statemenf of claim a medical report, substaintiating all the injuries and a statement of special damage. The statement of special damages claimed should include in the form of a schedule, not only particular of expenses and loesse already incurred, but also in estimate of any future expense and losses (including loss of earnings and pension rights). Its purpose is to enable the plaintiff to quantify his claim as fully and as early as possible. So that all parties know exactly where they stand at a very early stage and are able to decide what actions to take, such as whether to settle the claim or to make a payment into court.

(24) Negligent compensation case

A ship collided with a pier. The owners of the pier sued the master of the ship for damage, their generally endorsed writ only " negligent navigation". The plaintiff then discovered that the master's ticket had been granted on the basis of a certificate that was probably a " forgery".

The plaintiffs then served the statement of claim in which case of negligence. The trial result of dfendants were successful, it indicated that the reason, the defendants sought to have the statement of claim struck out on various grounds, including that it constituted a major departure from the allegation in the writ.

The purpose of the statement of claim is to set out the material facts of the case that establish the cause of action. It is not necessary to anticipate and attempt to respond to any defence that may be raised.

(25) Breach of damage contract case

The plaintiff householder sued the defendant builder for breach of contract for failing to complete work on the plaintiff's house. The defendant had a counterclaim that he sought to set off against the plaintiff's claim. The counterclaim could not be a legal set-off as it was " unliquidated", includine a claim on a ratio basis for payment for extra work done outside the contract and also for damages for defendant's tools.

Finally, the court of appeal held that the defendant had an equitbale set off which defeated the plaintiff's claim and gave judgement to the defendant on the claim,with costs and judgement to the defendant on counterclaim, with costs and judgement to the defendant on counterclaim again with costs. Hence, the plaintiff householder can not sue the denfentant builder for breach of contract for failing to complete work on the plaintiff's house successfully.

(26) Copyright infringerent claim civil case, product compensation case

A complaint by the defendant that the plaintiff had not pleaded adequate particulars of similarities between the copyright product and the infringing product failed after the court's visual examination failed after the court's visual examination of the two products some similarities were noted and thay are sufficient to sue copyright infringement claim successfully.

(27) Copyright infringerent claim civil case, drug compensation case

Injunctive relief means that high court ordinance with provides that the court of first instance may by order (whether interlocutory or final) grant an injunction in all cases in which it appears to the court of first instance to be just or convenient to do. An interlocutory injunction can only be granted against a party in proceedings where a substantive cause of action is asserted against party,such as a mandatory injunction compels the defendant to take the step specified in the order.

Constract a prohibitory injunction which restains the defendant from taking the specifc step case pharmaceutical company sought two forms of interlocutory relief. It is the plaintiff. The first as a prohibitory order, to the defendant

from continuing to publish a magazine bearing the commonly known Chinese name for one of the plaintiff company's well known drugs. This order was granted.
However the court refused to grant the second order sought, which was mandatory in nature to compel the defendant to deliver up any magazines or other publications in its possession, the distribution of which would be contrary to the restraining order.
The court took the view that the restraining order would adequately protect the plaintiff's interests. A mandatory injunction will only be ordered in exceptional cases and no good reason had been offered to demonstate that the case was an exceptional one.
An injunctive order that is interlocutory or temporary in nature, has effect until the trial of thhe action, whereas an interim injunction is effectively only until the hearing finishs. An injunction order that is of permanent, duration (a final injunctive is usually only granted after the trial of the action , although if (1) the parties gree and (2) there is no dispute between them concerning the facts. The court may treat an application for an interlocutory injunction as the actual trial of the action and make a final order.

(28) Permanent injunction to the principles for a petrol filling station licence compensation case

The plaintiffs owned a petrol filling station, they granted the defendants a licence to operate the filling station. The licence was allowed of one year's duration only. Once ir expired , the defendants continued to occupy the site. The defendants continued to occupy the site. The plaintiffs sought summary judgement for a permanent injunction to restrain the defendants from their trespass. The court, at first instance, found that the defendants has no arguable

case on the facts and summary judgement for an injunction was granted. The decision was uphead on appeal.
The purpose of an interlocutory injunction is to regulate the position between the parties until the full hearing of the substantive action. However , in practice many cases are concluded once the interlocutory injunction application has been heard. It is often the case that the outcome of the application for the interlocutory injunction is taken by the parties to be a strong indication for the ultimate result at trial, and the case is then settled, or alternatively, the interlocutory order sufficiently resolves the issue between the parties , so that there is no need to continue with the substantive action.

(29) Adequacy of damages to the plaintiff position case.

If the injunction is not granted , can the plaintiff's position adequately compensated later by an award of damages at trial? To demonstrate that an award of damages at the eventual trial of the action won't properly compensate the plaintiff of the application for an injunction is refused at this stage.
The plaintiff was a partner in a firm, she had been in dispute with her partnership firm on varous issues. Following a board meeting as managing partner of the office. The firm argued that she had handed in her notice. The defendant, partnership firm also disputed this on the ground that she had only threatened to resign. The notice partner was due to expire on Nov. . On 9 Oct. the plaintiff obtained a injunction to restrain the firm from acting in any way inconsistent with her rights or a partner . A week later, she applied for a continuation of the injunction to preserve her status as a partner and her ability to contribute to and share in profit of the office pending the outcome of

the dispute over her purported resignation. Her application was dismissed, the court deciding that damages would be an adequate compensation if the injunction were not continued . If she were successful in the main action, then it would be possible to quantify her "damage", which was purely financial in nature, consisting of her share of profit generated by the office.

(30) Interrogatories witness evidence case

Interrogatories are writtn questions, answered on oath or affirmation usually served after discovery of documents, seeking to clarify questions, relating to matters in issue between the parties and in cases. There are two forms: Interrogatories without order and order interrogatories. Interrogatories may be served without order on a party not more than twice. If the requesting party is not satisfied that the answers to interrogatories are sufficient, the requesting party may either seek further and better particulars of the answer given, or may apply for a court order requiring a further answer.

Parties are required to exchange written statements of the fact witnesses they intend to call. Arrangements for the exchange of witness statements are usually made at the hearing of the summons for directions or at the time that the matter is set doen for trial.

What is the position when a party wishes to call an unscheduled witness statements during the trial, no winess statement having been exchanged prior to the commencement of the trial?

During the trial, the plaintiff applied to the court to call one of their solicitors to give evidence. The reason given for the application was that the need to call the solicitor across purely out of new matters occuring during the trial . The court did not permit the calling of a witness who had not given a witness statement unless (1) there was good cause and (2) the court gave leave. On the particular facts, no good cause had been offered and leave was refused.

The witness statements will stand as the evidence in chief at the parties at trial , so that when the witness takes the advantages of dispensing with evidence in chief at the trial, the practice has received some judicial criticism in cases where the witness's reliability and credibility was in issue.

A witness statement should be comprehensive, cotaining all the evidence that the witness is able to adduce to prove the case of the party serving the statement. However, at the same time, it is important to ensure that the witness statement accurately records only the evidence that the witness is able to give.

There is no obligation on the person who serves he witness statement to call the witness at trial, and therefore there is no reason for the opposing party to assure that the witness will be called. We can contrast factevidence at trial by the party to whom the ansers were given.

What does expert evidence mean?

Expert evidence presented to the court to the expert, seen to be the independent product on the expert, uninfluenced as to form or content by the litigation.

A expert witness shoould provide independent assistance to the matters within his expertise. A expert witness should state the facts or assumption upon which his opinion is based. He should not omit to consider material facts which could detract from his concluded opinion. A expert witness should make it clear when a particular question or issue falls outside his expertise.

If an expert's opinion is not properly researched because he considers that insufficient data is vaiable, then this must be stated with an indication that the opinion is no more than a provisional one. In case, where an expert witness could not assert that the report contained the truth, the whole truth, and nothing but the truth, without some qualification, that qualification should be stated in the report.

If after exchange of reports, an expert witness changes his view on a material matter, having read the other side's expert's report or for any other reason, such change of view should be communicated to the other side without delay and when appropriate to the report. Where expert evidence refers to photographs, plans, survey reports or other similar documents, there must be provided to the opposite party at the same time as the exchange of reports.

(31) Written evidence for sale a flat contract case

The plaintiff sued the defendant for specific performance of contract for the plaintiff argued that the parties agreed, during a conversation in the lift lobby, the property , the parties and the price and they left to their solicitors all other formalities, including the completion date. The trial judge found that the plaintiff and the defendant had made a binding " open agreement" for the sale of the flat. The court of appeal made the decision. The court of final appeal allowed the defendant's appeal because:

(1) There were self-contradicatory findings of fact, the trial judge having stated that the contract sued on was an open contract, when at other points in the judgement having referred to a different contract as the one an which the suit was based.

(2) The existance of the open contract was not reflected or confirmed in any of the written material before the court, including the correspondence, and the pleading , or in the plaintiff's evidence at trial.

(3) It would be extremely unusual for two people to intend to make a binding contract for the sale of a flat in the

unanner suggested by the plaintiff and without any term as to time for completion.
In the result, the court of final appeal found that the only reasonable conclusion would be that the parties were negotiating and had made an agreement to agree.

(32) Appeal process in written evidence injured compensation case.

The plaintiff (employee) sued his employer (the UK construction firm) needed to compensate for his injured his back when at work. He made a claim for compensation , which his employer resisted. The employer demanded at trial that the plaintiff was lying about loss and when the accident occurred. The trial judge acknowedged that the plaintiff was not precise about dates, bute accepted his evidence and awarded over UK$400,000.00 . The employer appealed on the grounds that the plaintiff's story was concocted. The court of appeal refused to disturb the judge's decision. The employer had not crossed the very high applicable where findings of primary fact based on a judge's view of the credibility of a witness are challenged on appeal.

(33) Weight of the evidence for employee's blood clot disease in an accident at working environment compensation case

The plaintiff suffered a seizure during a tea break at work. He was later found to have a blood clot in the brain. He made a claim for employees' compensation. The blood clot was caused by a blow to the head that he suffered in an accident at work. There was no witnesses to the accident.
The trial judge approached the matter was one of rejected the appellant's evidence. The appellant challenged various findings of act on appeal. The appeal was dismissed, on the basis that there was no reason to disturb the trial. Judge's

findings, based as they were on the credibility and weight of th evidence at trial.

The judge's supporting reasons may include these factors as below:

There is no evidence to support the finding of fact or the finding of fact is contrary to related documentary or other evidence or the findings of fact could only have been based on a misapprehension of the facts, or on some other family process of reasoning.

(34) Seeking new evidence for dishonoured cheque defence case

The action on a dishonoured cheque, the defendant appealed to a judge for summary judgement, and attempted to introduce new evidence. The evidence related to the defence of failure of consideration, which was totally different to the defence that had been put forward before the judgement.

The judge exercised his discretion against admitting the evidence. The was not just a situation in which a party had discovered additional documents since th hearing before the judgement.

The defendant had changed its defence completely and the evidence had to be approached with caution. In the circumstances, it would be unfair to admit the new evidenece, so that the defendant could have another chance to advance a new denfence.

(35) Extending the time limits relevant to appeals the court of appeal for expert evidence case.

An assessement of damages trial is unread before a judgement. The plaintiff wishes an adduce additional expert evidence. The judgement refuses this request because it is made too late and the evidence is unnecessary

. The assessment continues and the judgement is made. The plaintiff is dissatisfied with the decision and decided to appeal. The refusal of the judgement to allow the additional expert evidence will be one of the grounds of appeal. The factors considered in deciding whether to grant the extension are the length of the delay, the reason for the delay, the chances of the appeal succeeding and the degree of prejudice to the defendant of extension of time is granted.

(36) Breach of copyright written evidence claim case.

The plaintiffs (students) prepared a questionnaire for use on an academic research project. The defendant on of their colleagues, was undertaking similar research and used part of their questionnaire in preparing his own questionnaire.

The plaintiffs succeed in their claim against the defendant for breach of copyright, and asked for costs on an ideminity basis becasue the defendant had failed to the existence of copyright, until the 40 th day of trial, and never have ownership of copyright, has admitted facts on cross-examination of the trial that he had refused to admit in response to a notice to admit, and had given misleading answers in response.

The court found that the defendant's conduct, when it had unreasonably added very considerably to the time and therefore the costs, which had to be spent on case preparation and the trial. Costs on a common fund basis were ordered.

(37) Defendant's video recorded for his interview with plaintiff unnecessary evidence claim case

The defendant's (staff) medical expert in a personal injury case had video-recorded his interview with the plaintiff (employer) and had prepared his report with reference to the video recorded interview. In fact, the staff did not know that their interview process between medical expert and him , which is recorded by video.

The report was therefore not in the accepted form. The judge to whom the matter was referred by the master found that the interview process would be recorded, that the plaintiff's informed consent was not obtained and that the defendants had made erroneous submissions to the judge as to precendents for the admissibility of such reports. The judge stated that the practice of video-recording interviews was ordered to pay the costs of the plaintiff on a common fund basis, and those costs were determined by gross sum assessment.

9 798887 830629

Printed by Libri Plureos GmbH in Hamburg,
Germany